MESSAGE OF BIBLICAL SPIRITUALITY
Editorial Director: Carolyn Osiek, RSCJ

Volume 8

The Gospel
of
Matthew

Miriam Perlewitz, M.M.

Michael Glazier
Wilmington, Delaware

ABOUT THE AUTHOR

After serving as missioner for ten years in the Far East, Miriam Perlewitz received a M.A. and Ph.D. in Biblical Languages and Literature in 1977 from St. Louis University Divinity School. Since then, she has been Professor of Biblical Studies at the Maryknoll Graduate School of Theology, and has participated in renewal programs for missioners and New York archdiocesan programs for adults.

Library of Congress Cataloging-in-Publication Data

Perlewitz, Miriam.
  Gospel of Matthew.

  (Message of biblical spirituality; v. 8)
    1. Bible. N.T. Matthew—Criticism, interpretation,
etc. 2. Spirituality—Biblical teaching. I. Title.
II. Series.
BS2575.2.P43   1988   226'.206   88-82467
ISBN 0-89453-558-7
ISBN 0-89453-574-9 (pbk.)

Message of Biblical Spirituality series:
0-89453-500-1, Cloth; 0-89453-566-8, Paper

Typography by Phyllis Boyd LeVane
Printed in the United States of America.

In Gratitude for my
PARENTS AND BROTHERS
who have taught me by
their faithfulness.

TABLE OF CONTENTS

EDITOR'S PREFACE

One of the characteristics of church life today is a revived interest in spirituality. There is a growing list of resources in this area, yet the need for more is not exhausted. People are yearning for guidance in living an integrated life of faith in which belief, attitude, affections, prayer, and action form a cohesive unity which gives meaning to their lives.

The biblical tradition is a rich resource for the variety of ways in which people have heard God's call to live a life of faith and fidelity. In each of the biblical books we have a witness to the initiative of God in human history and to the attempts of people not so different from ourselves to respond to the revelation of God's love and care.

The fifteen volumes in the *Message of Biblical Spirituality* series aim to provide ready access to the treasury of biblical faith. Modern social science has made us aware of how the particular way in which one views reality conditions the ways in which one will interpret experience and life itself. Each volume in this series is an attempt to retell and interpret the biblical story from within the faith perspective that originally formed it. Each seeks to portray what it is like to see God, the world, and oneself from a particular point of view and to search for ways to respond faithfully to that vision. We who are citizens of our twentieth century world cannot be people of the ancient biblical world, but we can grow closer to their experience and their faith and thus closer to God, through the living Word of God which is the Bible.

The series includes an international group of authors representing England, Ireland, Canada, and the United States, but whose life experience has included first-hand knowledge of many other countries. All are proven scholars and committed believers whose faith is as important to them as their scholarship. Each acts as interpreter of one part of the biblical tradition in order to enable its spiritual vitality to be passed on to others. It is our hope that through their labor the reader will be able to enter more deeply into the life of faith, hope, and love through a fuller understanding of and appreciation for the biblical Word as handed down to us by God's faithful witnesses, the biblical authors themselves.

Carolyn Osiek, RSCJ
Associate Professor of New Testament Studies
Catholic Theological Union, Chicago

Background

The goal of the Gospel of Matthew is the goal of every writer of a spirituality, that is, to make the Word and the Person of Jesus as present and alive today as he was two thousand years ago. The message of Matthew is a message of faith. It is set down in a series of discourses on the old expectations of Israel and their new fulfillment embodied in Jesus. It is a message with deep implications.

To situate Matthew's message of faith, we must understand the historical setting and the situation of the Jewish Christian community of his day. The Gospel is addressed to a Jewish Christian community around the year 85 A.D., when the Jerusalem temple and the city were destroyed and the Jews themselves were exiled from their homeland. The Jewish rebellion of 70 A.D. which caused this diaspora existence was prompted by messianic beliefs and hopes. The Pharisees, the sect of the Jewish community that survived the war against the Roman Empire, set up a new center of worship in Jamnia, a city on the Mediterranean coast. It was there that the Pharisees continued to foster their messianic hopes. There they waited. With utter optimism the Pharisaic community expected their return to the Holy Land, the crumbling of foreign domination and the extermination of their oppressors. They believed that these events would usher in the kingdom of the messiah. In these circumstances the Jewish Christians found themselves subject to messianic expectations that they could not accept in conscience. They could not join in the struggle for deliverance. For them, Jesus was the Messiah, the Savior and the fulfillment of Israel's hopes and expectations.

At this time the Jewish Christian community was also suffering from isolation from synagogue worship. Furthermore, they were overwhelmed by the influx of Gentile believers. It had always been a tenet of Israel's religious belief that to be holy people of God it was essential for them to be set apart. Christian belief was transforming the human condition and resulting in some radical insights into the heart of Israel's tradition and Law. Jews and Gentiles were now free to worship in unity. Roman and Jewish authorities were continually harassing the Jewish Christian community. All these factors caused tension and division both within and outside the community. For the community there were also many practical questions: Who is to be accepted into the community? Who are the believers? Who are the people of God, the recipients of the promises given to Abraham and David? What is to be done about the Law and the Prophets? Are the traditions of the elders to be followed or the teachings of Jesus? These questions and concerns, however, focused on the externals of their religious beliefs. They failed to penetrate into the heart of the faith, that God is present in the human condition in Jesus and through Jesus; God's Wisdom Incarnate.

This book is one possible interpretation of the spirituality of Matthew's Gospel. There are many others. It is not meant to be a commentary on but a companion to Matthew's Gospel. It is to be read and to be reflected upon in conjunction with the message delivered by Matthew to his community of believers.

The themes flow from the structure of the Gospel and follow the plan of Matthew's own instructions. This is a book about the faith of the Jewish Christians, the faith which is of the essence of the spiritual life. Some will pick up this book, leaf through it and then put it down; others will read it to the end, hopefully. Those who do may find a story reflective of their own personal lives, for Matthew tells us that this story is indeed our own.

In Matthew's Gospel faith is not merely believing in something or someone, even if the person is Jesus. Faith is not adherence to a doctrine or a definition about Jesus' life or how Jesus functions in this community of believers. The faith that Jesus speaks about in Matthew's Gospel is a call to a radically new existence. Jesus himself lived it and exemplified it. It is a faith that demands looking at our very life, our humanness, our personal commitment to God at its roots, at its source, at its core in light of Jesus's message. To live by faith and not by sight, to live with the insight of faith that God is with us in Jesus, Risen and Lord of the world, is to create an environment and home, a place of peace, harmony and forgiveness on earth—as it is in heaven—this is wisdom.

But who is this Matthew, this Christian at heart, who is able to see beyond the limits of the perception of the human condition to the unlimited horizon that faith holds out to all who believe in God revealed to us in Jesus?

Matthew may have been a tax collector who had been ostracized from the Jewish community because of his public office. Persons who held the position of tax collector had the reputation of doing business illegally and thereby corrupting the community's image and good name. In the traditional religious observances of Judaism, the law did not permit the Jews to associate with the class of people known as the tax collectors and/or sinners.

We do not know for certain but Matthew may even have been a Gentile, an outsider, a foreigner, admitted into the community of believers sometime after the death and resurrection of Jesus. The specific name and background of the person of Matthew are not all that vital for hearing and understanding the message of Jesus.

Of one thing we may be sure, Matthew the believer, whether of Jewish or Gentile ancestry, knew what it meant to be forgiven. It is this message of spirituality that is evident from his Gospel account. Matthew was drawn in mind and heart to Jesus, the Risen Lord of his life. Matthew's instructions on the compassionate love and forgiving ministry of Jesus to the community residing outside of Palestine, perhaps in Antioch, Syria, are masterful indeed.

Faith is what the four Gospels are all about. Each shows that faith is the dynamic relationship we have with God through reliance upon Jesus, his word and his way. Matthew is concerned with showing the integrative union of the ancestral traditions of Judaism with the person of Jesus and the Christian community for all time. He begins and ends his Gospel with the assurance: "God-with-us" in Jesus remains with us as Risen Lord until the end of time; God comes to us in our humanness and relates to us according to the quality of our relationships with one another; God comes to save us from our sin. God reminds the Jews that a change of mind and heart is necessary to see the kingdom of "God-with-us." This is the critical message of forgiveness. If we believe that Jesus is with us today then, "Whatever you do to the least of these my brothers and sisters, you do to me" (Matt 25:40). Negatively stated it is even more emphatic: "As you did it not to one of the least of these, you did it not to me" (Matt 25:45).

1

Presence:
The Fulfillment of Israel's Expectations
(Matt 1-2)

The Dilemma of Believers

Numerous generations of women and men consistently believed in the promise given to them by God through their ancestors, who formally covenanted a special relationship with God:

> "I will establish my covenant between me and you and your descendants after you throughout their generations for an everlasting covenant, to be God to you and to your descendants after you. And I will give to you, and to your descendants after you, the land of your sojournings; all the land of Canaan, for an everlasting possession; and I will be their God" (Gen 17:7f).

At the time Matthew was writing, a new phenomenon took place. The descendants of Israel believed God but not all believed in the fulfillment of the covenant in Jesus. None of Israel's hopes for this covenant relationship was fulfilled in the way she had anticipated. This is the dilemma.

Throughout the centuries Israel's hopes took on a variety of forms and expressions. In the religious dialogue between God and his People the expectations of a homeland, numerous descendants and prosperity were continually changing. God's covenant promise alone remained constant and sure.

Even though the word "promise" does not occur in Matthew's Gospel, the entire history of God's relationship with the people Israel is dependent upon the "Word of God." In times past God had spoken many times and in many ways through the Law and the Prophets. What is noteworthy about Matthew's Gospel is that he demonstrates clearly that God has already fulfilled the promise to Israel.The word of God is a personal, dynamic, living word as spoken through the prophets (Matt 1:22; 2:5, 15, 17, 23).

Isn't it extraordinary that the "word of God" or the "promise of God" appear in the singular throughout the Scriptures! Can we not extrapolate a special significance from this fact. In Matthew's Gospel the promise is Jesus. Jesus is the critical message of God incarnated. Jesus is God's unique response, God's gift that fulfills all the hopes and expectations of Israel and all our hopes as well. God has given his word to Israel.

Matthew opens his gospel with a genealogy which introduces Jesus Christ and identifies him as son of Abraham and son of David (Matt 1:1). Matthew also identifies the community of believers. The believers are those who claim the inheritance of Abraham and the house of David. The simple purpose of the genealogy is to introduce the community of believers of both Jews and Gentiles to their common heritage; the promise made to Abraham, to David and to the fourteen generations in exile. The genealogy also implicitly illustrates the continuity of God's promise and the expectation of believers throughout the generations.

Dominant in chapters 1 and 2 are the unexpected ways in which God fulfills his promise and the inconsistent and varied response of the believers. The Infancy narratives tell the story. There is no judgment or indictment of past generations.

THE PROMISE TO ABRAHAM

The first generation of believers consistently believed that they would become a great nation, and have prosperity on the land; but they lacked continuity in their roots. The believers were not all members of the race and tribes of Israel. Many who cooperated in fulfilling the promise to Abraham failed to conform to the laws set down by the tribes to maintain the purity of ancestral lineage. The promise of God to Abraham was brought about in great part by women and men of foreign descent and sometimes with irregularities in their relationships. Their belief was consistent; their racial inheritance was mixed.

THE PROMISE TO DAVID

The second set of fourteen generations of believers lived during the period of the monarchy. Although the tradition of the Law and the Prophets was central to their lives, they were not always faithful to the Law in practice. The Book of Kings informs us that the monarchs were judged faithful or un-faithful, just or unjust before God, in accord with their observance of the Law. Despite their infidelity, the kings were privy to the promise of God given to David and his house (Matt 1:7-11): "Your house and your kingdom shall be made sure forever before me; your throne shall be established forever" (II Sam 7:16). Paradoxically, when the kingdom was destroyed and the prophets perished, Israel continued to believe that the kingdom promised to David would be established forever.

The third set of fourteen generations of believers were expelled from their homeland, the land of promise, and lived in exile. Despite alienation and separation, despite their living in a foreign land, these chosen people were filled with hope and expectation of their return and the fulfillment of the promise of God (Matt 1:12-16). Israel continued to believe God's word of promise to them and this faith bore the fruit of God's Promised One, the Messiah . . . "Jacob, the father of Joseph, the husband of Mary of whom Jesus was born, who is called Christ" (Matt 1:16).

The word of the Lord spoken to the patriarchs and the prophets was not spoken in vain. The promise of God is consistent, yet it is expressed in various forms and fulfilled in totally unexpected ways: "Behold, a virgin shall conceive and bear a son and shall call his name Emmanuel" (Matt 1:23; Isa 7:14). The promise is fulfilled in a radically new way. Mary's child is given the name Jesus (Savior), and the throne name of the Son of God (Emmanuel) is interpreted "God-with-us" (Matt 1:23).

The Dilemma of Believers in Jesus

The inimitable promise challenges the individuals and the community of believers to respond. In retrospect, we see the salvation events in the lives of the people of Israel, reenacted in the life of Jesus. What has happened in the life of Jesus may happen also in the lives of believers.

JOSEPH THE JUST MAN

The word of God in the form of the Mosaic Law was a key factor in the lives of the Jewish people at the time of Jesus' birth. The law restricted Joseph from taking Mary, who was with child of the Holy Spirit, for his lawful wife.

Joseph, the believer, a faithful observer of the Mosaic Law, reflected upon the word of God in his heart and responded in fidelity to God and to Mary. (Angelic and dream visions are expressions for the various forms of personal encounter with God). Joseph, the just man, had transgressed the Law by Jewish standards or the Pharisaic criterion of justice. And yet he believed God.

In earnest we ask the question: Does Joseph's action circumvent the Law of God? Is Joseph truly a just man? Is Joseph truly faithful? But these questions are our concerns. The purpose of Matthew's teaching is to reiterate for his community, God's fulfillment of his promise. Jesus is son of Mary but essentially he is Son of God. The human and the divine meet. The heavenly is incarnated in this world, in history. God is faithful indeed.

THE WISE MEN

The Magi came from pagan lands to worship the child born king of the Jews. A star, nature's cosmic sign, revealed and interpreted the birth of a divine ruler. It is through the Gentile race and universal symbols, that the Jews, "Herod and all Jerusalem with him" (Matt 2:3), receive the good news verified by their Scriptures. "A ruler has been sent by God to shepherd the people Israel" (cf. Matt 2:6; II Sam 5:2; I Chr 11:2).

The Magi were the first to recognize and worship the promised Messiah, the expected ruler, the king of the Jews. Thus, the Gentiles became the first believers. What is the message for Matthew's community? Why was it so difficult for the Jewish believers to recognize the promise of God fulfilled in this child? Does power lie dormant within the innocence of a child? Does this child threaten a believer's image of God?

IN EXILE AND RETURN

Herod responds to the historical event by plotting to destroy the life of the divine child. Conversely, the Magi thwart the plan and are instrumental in saving the life of the child Jesus, whose mission as Savior is to save Israel from her sins (Matt 1:21).

In this situation Joseph responds by reflecting on the word of the Lord to him. Joseph takes the child and his mother and flees to Egypt. The land of exile for the Israelites becomes the place of salvation and refuge for the Savior. The Holy Family settles there until the death of Herod when it is safe to return to the promised land. However, the continued threat on Jesus' life results in Joseph, Mary and the child Jesus taking up residence in Nazareth, the land of the Gentiles. The prophecies of old are consistently fulfilled in Israel; but it is inconsistent with Israel's expectations that the innocent ones should suffer and die in the struggle for the life of the believers (Matt 2:18; Jer 31:15). This theme is played out consistently throughout the Gospel; the inconsistency is played out once again in the end. The death of the innocent one, Jesus, brings forth new life (Matt 26-28).

Matthew clarifies for us and for the Jewish-Gentile Christian community what it means to be a believer. We rely on the promises of God to Abraham, to David and to the generations in exile. We rely on those who continue to believe and to hope when all signs of assurance and expectation seem to fail. We rely on the people who have gone before, who have lived and died in exile in anticipation of a future time and place when there would be peace and justice on this earth. As a Christian community we stand in continuity with this tradition.

But then we must ask: Have Israel's hopes and expectations been realized? Are our hopes and expectations only too similar? Do we still look to the future for a witness of peace and justice in this world? Does the Jesus of Matthew's Gospel speak a message of hope fulfilled and of hope yet to be realized for the community of the Church today? Is Jesus of Nazareth meaningful for the men and women of today? Is Jesus real enough for us to see our hopes fulfilled in the present?

Israel was consistent in her desires to respond to God, to become a people who listened and heard the word of God. But Israel sought her identity as a people in the land and in the kingdom. *Things* intervened in the relationship between God and Israel. Material or earthly realities may stand as idols between God and the human person. We all believe in some *thing* or some *one.* As human beings we have the capacity to see and hear what is heavenly in earthly realities. We are free to choose. Would we trade God's presence for things? Can we be a people of God without land and/or institutions? Do people of God consistently turn to idols? Anything that stands in the way of a direct heartfelt response to God, is an idol.

The number and races of peoples, the land, the kingdom, the religious signs, symbols and practices have been recast in our day. In the future when all external forms, concrete hopes and images pass away, the ultimate *word*, the promise of God will remain: "I will be with you always" (Matt 28:20).

The promise is ONE—"God-with-us!" The promise is not the *things* that we had hoped for, the materialities of our earthly existence. The true sum and substance of our existence in this world is to be a people of God, to be just and righteous before God, self and all others; to be that presence of God in the world as individual and as community; to listen and to be bold to speak the word of God, 'the still, small voice' within us.

As believers we bear this greatest of expectations. As believers we consistently hope in this promise and are aware, too, that the promise of God may be fulfilled in ways that are utterly inconsistent with our ways of seeing and hearing. To see "God-with-us" in the child Jesus is revolutionary and requires the greatest act of faith. To be open to see and hear that the promise is fulfilled in this new and unexpected event is essentially what it means to be a believer.

To live with the assurance that God is, indeed, present with us, whether Jew or Gentile, is what it means to live in faith: to *be in* God's presence. Emmanuel "God-with-us" is the kingdom promised to David, the land, and the community, and the security that Abraham expected. All that we have ever hoped for and expected is a reality now and in the future, in and through Jesus. This is the magnificent dilemma we also face as believers.

2

Presence:
The Fulfillment of God's Expectations
(Matt 3-4)

Transition

An invitation is extended to the Jewish community: "Repent, the kingdom of heaven is at hand" (Matt 3:2; 4:17). The prophetic word of John the Baptist and Jesus announces the good news to those who are willing to accept the presence of God with them. Matthew begins the passage with "In those days." These words usher in a new age and a time of change. What is needed to make a change from oppression to freedom, from slavery to liberation or salvation? What is needed to make the transition from the old age to the new age in an apparently unchanged social situation? The age of transition calls for repentance. Repentance is a remembrance of God's promise and God's activity on behalf of Israel through past generations. But repentance is more than reflection on the past; repentance requires a remembrance of God's faithfulness in the past, a remembrance that can effect a change of mind and heart in the present.

A TIME OF EXPECTATION

"In those days" (Matt 3:1)—Matthew specifies an era when God's expectations, made known by the word of promise are fulfilled. Israel was entering an age of relationship with God unlike any other previous time in history. "In those days" particularizes the time when believers encounter the presence of God in Jesus. This period of time, when the expectations of Israel are finally realized, demands repentance that engages us in a life-long process.

A time of expectation designates a time of waiting and hoping. What are the expectations of Israel in relationship to God? In Matthew's community it was known as a time when the kingdom of God's presence and rule would be experienced on earth as it assuredly is in heaven. We often speak of it as a time of salvation. But what we are saved *from* and what we are saved *for* requires explanation. Our expectations may be many and varied but basically they come down to one ultimate truth: we desire to be free to live our lives in the company of God, of self and of others with peace and happiness all the days of our life.

Repentance

A TIME OF CHANGE (Matt 3:1-12)

John the Baptist comes from the desert to the Jordan and announces the time of God's expectation. The time of deliverance is at hand. Repent!

The Greek word metanoia is used frequently by the Church and represents the concept of repentance or conversion. We are simply to turn from our old ways and turn toward God. This has been the predominant interpretation. In recent times, it has become more common and more accurate to translate the word metanoia from its etymological base: (NOIA) nous or mind, with the prefix (META) change. The English word metamorphosis indicates a change of form. The word metanoia, translated as repentance, indicates a change of mind.

This interpretation is critical for the insight into Matthew's Gospel as a spiritual way of life. A change of mind and heart ostensibly changes the old patterns of revelation in life, but repentance is also required to see the new revelation of the presence of "God-with-us" in Jesus. The rule of sin and rebellion no longer holds sway. Our minds and hearts give full power and dominion to the rule of God. It is a time of transformation; a time of deliverance; a time of metanoia. Repentance is the ground and seed bed for a new perspective on life. Repentance is necessary to perceive and accept God's presence and not to judge the present by our standards of judgments from the past. In accord with tradition, judgments of good and evil were instituted by the legal requirements of the Law.

John and Jesus proclaim repentance as a necessity to accept "God-with-us" in the present, and to free us from judging present events by our standards of good and evil. Repentance functions through the eye of faith as a filter for seeing and coping with change. As a prelude to the Sermon on the Mount, repentance prepares the community to hear the teachings of Jesus on God's justice and God's judgment.

A TIME OF BAPTISM (Matt 3:13-16)

The prophetic announcement heralded "In those days" as a time of purifying Israel's way of life. It allowed her to live out her hopes and desires to permit God to act in and through her. It required a change in Israel's estimate of herself as a community of believers. As John the Baptist recounts: Jesus, the superior one comes to the inferior. This time advocates a reversal of roles and a change in the established hierarchical order.

The leadership of the community, the persons of the Pharisees and Sadducees come to John to be baptized. John exposed their dubious intent and purpose for baptism. "Who has warned you to flee from the wrath to come?" (Matt 3:7). Wrath is a symbolic word for destruction and judgment at the end of time.

Baptism is the ritual sign of God's deliverance from the end-time judgment now in the present time. To flee from this "wrath to come" involves more than the external, symbolic action. The sacred sign, baptism, the essential being of the one who enters into this way of repentance, requires a lifetime witness to actions that are not judgmental. Repentance befits the one who stands in a relationship with God and allows God to be God.

Israel may fear the judgment of God in the future but Israel also needs a baptism of repentance. Baptism without the change of mind and heart, without the change of attitude that permeates actions and good deeds, can have no meaning or significance for a life of faith. Jews and Gentiles, as believers, are all children of Abraham. Believers whose expectations and blessings have come through Jesus, share in the same relationship as children of the one God. It is important, therefore, that life bring forth fruit that fulfills justice. Justice is what we do with our lives, how we live our lives in relationship to a God who can create and destroy; a God who uproots and plants; a God who puts minds and hearts under question and asks us to reflect on our ancestral forebears. Are blood ties or family relationships the only criterion for believers? Does water-baptism or ritual purity make us repentant? Is it sufficient to go through the fire of Holy Spirit baptism without producing the fruits of a good life, a life where the Spirit motivates the actions and the judgment is left to God alone who, in the end, sees and judges minds and hearts?

A TIME OF REVELATION (Matt 3:17-19)

A time of revelation is a time of rethinking our relationships to and our understanding of God who is with us. The promised one moves from a place of synagogue to church. Our status symbols and standard views of a God-act have to be reconsidered. Jesus undergoes baptism of repentance for sin; his association with the human condition fulfills all justice. The fulfillment of God's will in Jesus' life was the purpose of baptism as well as the message: the person and the content, the "coming ONE" the Messiah, the anointed ONE is present. All Israel's expectations of God are exploded. Jesus is not a fiery reformer. Jesus appears as all other people, humble and of highest moral conduct. God's acknowledgment of him as Son "beloved" and only one, the suffering servant, reveals to us the model of believers and the response that we are to make.

The Father grants a sign of Jesus' sonship by bestowing the Holy Spirit, and once again we are asked to reflect on the ways of God.

A TIME OF WILDERNESS EXPERIENCE (Matt 4:1-11)

"In those days" is a time of testing of our relationship as children of God; a time of rethinking our understanding of the promised one. Jesus' sonship was tested and to be believers requires that we question our relationship with God.

The wilderness or desert seems an apt image to describe the doubt and the questioning that arises in our minds and hearts. "Taken up" by the Spirit, our minds and hearts experience ecstasy and justice (Matt 4:1). This is the wilderness experience. Justice flows from ecstasy and allows our actions to confirm what and how we see!

Since the Messiah, Jesus, has come, the period of the end-time blessing or gift has been given. Jesus is the in-breaking of the presence of God in our midst. This is why the message of salvation that is preached by John and reiterated by Jesus bears such a powerful impact on our lives. A change of mind is needed to be able to see the kingdom of heaven at hand. Jesus, the presence of God, is the very gift and reality of the kingdom come.

(1) *Stones into Bread*

This personal presence of God in our midst is not without its temptations. Just as Jesus in the desert experienced the torment and questioning regarding his sonship, so do we also doubt and question our own identity as children of God. To be able to accept this relationship to God in faith, requires that we transcend the choices of this world's concept of honor, prestige and fate. The offer of power and authority over the things of this world is one temptation that is not easily overcome. Attractive job-offers and responsibilities can easily carry us away in fantasy and illusions that we truly are *great*. But the voice within us can be heard faintly and persistently: God is Lord and God alone is to be worshipped.

(2) Nations for Our Inheritance

A second cause for testing and doubt is the apparent need that we have to prove by our words that we are "gifted." Faith is intended to make us a "wonder-worker" of sorts and, according to the teaching of Jesus, we are to move mountains if we have faith even as small as a mustard seed (Matt 17:20f.; 21:22). What does it mean to have faith? What does it mean to bear this filial relationship with God? Does it empower us? Does it allow us to assist and aid others in our journey to the goal of our existence? Jesus was able to satisfy the multitudes with bread just as Moses fed the Israelites in the desert, but Jesus weighed the consequences of performing this deed for his own sake. The basic conditions for the miracles of faith are the needs of the suffering and the poor who have no food.

(3) True/False Relationships

The third opportunity for changing our mind about our role and function as children of God is to pass the test of trust in our future fate. We may not know what the future brings but we are prepared for the consequences of a faith-life which allows God to save us within the way we will live out our life. To subject ourselves to danger for the sake of proving God's presence with us, would be jeopardizing our faith stance. Faith is a way of life with Jesus that goes along the way of darkness and the unknown. Wherever that road leads us will be the path of our salvation and our light. It is no longer faith when we direct and plan and put ourselves in danger of falling into the brink of disaster or despair.

Although we have faith and experience the presence of God in Jesus, we are still subject to temptations and doubt and fears. But the proclamation of Jesus is a reminder to us: "Change your mind: the kingdom of heaven is at hand."

A TIME OF FULFILLMENT (Matt 4:12-17)

"In those days" is known as the time of deliverance. Deliverance has a particular meaning in Matthew's Gospel. Its breaking point culminates in the passion narrative where Jesus is delivered or handed over in his passion and death to be restored to the fullness of life at his resurrection. The outcome is decisive. Deliverance is a handing over of the fullness of life through death and we are the beneficiaries. John the Baptist is "handed over" as the last of the prophets of the old age. The time when God revealed his word and his will through prophecy has come to an end. The age of prophecy ceases. God reveals his will in Jesus. God's word is spoken anew in the person of Jesus who reveals God "In those days . . ." mythic time. It is not the end of time. It is the time of the end to all that inhibits us from seeing and hearing God and knowing his will for us. It is a time of deliverance to the powers of God or the powers of this world. John the Baptist is "handed over" to the destructive forces of this world. Jesus then moves into Galilee, the land of the Gentiles, to minister to his people's needs. He is in exile, so to speak, from his own land. He is with people thought to be in the shadowland, a kingdom thought to be in darkness and death in a politically oppressive state, a kingdom where the Romans hold power and dominion. It is here that Jesus begins his ministry.

We are called upon to change our mind, to repent (Matt

4:17) to rethink our concepts of land, peoples, kingdom and darkness. What value is the earth to our existence? Is the place where we reside a determining factor in our life? Who essentially are the believers? Where is the kingdom of heaven that proclaims Jesus as king/ruler here and hereafter? When is darkness turned to light? Does it take effect in time and space? Is it an external factor or an internal gift? When do we see darkness over the land, peoples, kingdoms? Is it because the light or the sun does not appear each day? Or is the darkness within our earthly sheol (depths of being), a religiously darkened state that prohibits us from perceiving the light of life that has dawned upon us (Matt 4:16; Isa 9:2d)?

A TIME OF GOD'S PRESENCE IN JESUS (Matt 4:18-25)

"In those days" is the time when Jesus brings the age of new life and light and inaugurates the kingdom. "Change your mind: the kingdom of heaven is at hand" (Matt 4:17). Jesus comes to assume definitive rule over the world (Matt 4:23-25). He calls us to follow, to participate in his ministry to the world. Anything that prevents us from living in union with God, that inhibits life with God, self, or others is healed (forgiven). This is the ministry of Jesus. His authoritative word creates discipleship as well. The model of discipleship is set before us in the first four persons who are called: "Immediately they left their nets and followed Jesus" (Matt 4:20). For those who have a change of mind and heart, this is possible.

In summary, repentance is not a once-and-for-all conversion process. We can see from the period of time known as "those days" that it is a continual process that requires a rethinking, redefining, a reminding of ourselves that God does not see our world, people, lands, kingdom as we see them. There is a different way of looking at this world; it is the place of the presence of God. If we could but see the world in this light! This is the work and the quest of a lifetime. It requires repentance to cope with change.

In those days presents us with a time of reassessing our faith in relationship to God in and through Jesus. "Those days . . ." (Matt 3:1) reflects a time of expectation; a time of repentance, baptism and confession of sin; a time of revelation of the *promised one* who then is tested regarding his sonship. It is a time of the kingdom when the presence of God is fulfilled by Jesus becoming one with us.

Those days leads us to the temptation to risk our lives, to test our worth and our powers. This can lead to destruction or to salvation. The true self and the false self both vie with one another on this road to the kingdom. But the path to the kingdom of heaven is one of suffering and the cross. The path to the kingdom of this earth is a victory we win for ourselves. There are two types of response, two powers within us. "We will have the nations for our inheritance," whispers the voice of the self, or we will have God's kingdom for our inheritance. The invitation comes to us in the words of Jesus.

The voice of the Spirit presents the view of the promised land, the view of the promised kingdom, and the voice of the "self" encourages us to rise and conquer these worlds that share dominion with us. But the voice of the Spirit in the relationship of faith calls for a surrender of these grandiose ideas of power and authority and rule and ownership. The victory of heaven and earth, the victory of the Spirit over temptation makes the question of our relationship with God and self and the promised One a choice and a surrender. "In those days" is mythic time.

3

Presence:
The Fulfillment of the Law
and Prophetic Expectations
(Matt 5-7)

Do Justice

Matthew explains, through the discourse of the Sermon on the Mount, that the teachings of Jesus are not in opposition to those of Judaism; they are in continuity with them. Jesus and his followers shared the same ancestral traditions of the Fathers: the Torah and the Prophets, as well as the Wisdom writings. The Old Testament Scripture inspired and guided the followers of Jesus in living out their Christian inheritance, their relationship to Jesus in a Jewish context. The same message of the Law and the Prophets is critical for hearing and understanding the teachings of Jesus. Jesus did not come to bring a new Law but the fulfillment of justice. He presented the community of the Jewish Christians with a new insight into their expectations of the messianic kingdom.

Jesus announces, "I have not come to abolish the Law and the Prophets but to fulfill them" (Matt 5:17). For Matthew, the person and the word of Jesus function as the paradigm for the Sermon on the Mount. Now that Jesus is present to the world as Risen Lord, the message of the Law and the Prophets is fulfilled and a new form of justice is required. Consequently, Matthew reiterates the teaching of Jesus: "Unless your justice exceeds that of the Scribes and the Pharisees you shall never enter the kingdom of heaven" (Matt 5:20). The presence of Jesus, his entire life and teachings, constitute the new model of justice. The Sermon on the Mount summarizes this teaching as follows: "Whatsoever you desire others do to you, do to them, for this is the Law and the Prophets" (Matt 7:12). These words of Jesus offer a message of spirituality for all time: do and teach (cf. Matt 5:19).

Justice, or righteousness in some translations, assumes central significance in the Sermon on the Mount (Matt 5:3, 10; 6:1, 33; 7:21). It is not a new teaching. Justice is constitutive of the message of the Scriptures and embraces the entire way of life of the people Israel. Justice is a way of life that accepts all of created existence as a gift from God, to be received with gratitude and to be dispensed with generosity. Justice encompasses all ordered activity and ethical behavior before God, humankind, animal life and all relationships with the cosmic forces of nature. There is nothing in life that is untouched by justice. It encompasses the activity of human beings but also designates the activity of God. Justice is both legal and social. It constitutes ethical uprightness, covenant-loyalty, obedience to the Torah, as expressive of God's will. It determines the persons who love and speak the good and the true.

Justice is relational as well as forensic and reflects God's very own activity along these same lines. God judges justly, acts justly, speaks what is right, vindicates and saves us by delivering us from what destroys us or destroys life. God is the God who saves. This is justice with its divine and human counterpart.

Justice is essentially and primarily God's gift to us, the gift of life and salvation. Because the ordered and right relationship of humankind with God has become disordered, justice has now been designated a characteristic of the new age. Where human justice is wanting, the search for God's intervention arises. The believer knows that the justice of God will endure. When justice is present, God is present.

What particular aspect of justice does Matthew stress for the Jewish Christian community? The justice that Jesus requires is rooted in the same teachings of the Law and the Prophets, but the true justice of God is embodied now in the wisdom of Jesus' life/teaching.

THE TEACHINGS OF JESUS IN THE SERMON
(Matt 5-7)

Each section of the Sermon on the Mount treats justice, or the one reality of life in this world, from a dual perspective. There are two ways of perceiving reality; there are two ways of observing the Law; two ways of exercising justice; two ways of entering the kingdom. The traditional Jewish approach requires one to live justly according to the Law or Torah based on the teachings of the Scribes and the Pharisees. The alternate approach to the Law, which Matthew describes, is the charter of the Christian life as it is set forth in the person and the word of Jesus.

With creative insight Matthew teaches the Jewish Christian community that the law of the Gentiles (Wisdom) and the Jewish Torah are one and the same. Both are the Law of God: Matthew equates wisdom with Law, and justice with Law. In the Sermon on the Mount, Jesus goes to the heart of Law and touches the heart of the human person. There he reveals that wisdom is justice and that justice resides both in the divine and the human spirit. To be just is wisdom because the way of the wise is justice. "Seek first the kingdom and God's justice and all things will be given to you as well" (Matt 6:33). This is the teaching of Jesus for the Jews and the Gentiles.

WISDOM AS LAW

Prior to giving the gift of the Law, God bestowed upon humankind the gift of life and wisdom. The law is a guide in the way to God but it does not supersede the word of God that is heard by the wise in the depth of the human heart. This voice of conscience or the spirit is wisdom in dialogue with the Law's expectation; it is the only true court of appeal. In the integral union of mind and heart and deed with God's will, "God-with-us" speaks.

TWO WAYS OF OBSERVING LAW (Matt 5:21-48)

The lead line of the teaching on the Mosaic Law reads "You have heard" or "It was said" (Matt 5:21, 27, 31, 33, 38, 43). Jesus responds to this teaching with the authoritative statement: "But I say to you" or "Amen I say to you" (Matt 5:22, 26, 28, 32, 34, 39, 44). The two types of observances are placed in antithetical parallelism: the Jewish way and the Christian way. In Matthew's community, believers both Jew and Gentile compare and perhaps even compete in their just duties before God. There are external similarities in the fulfillment of the requirements of the Law but there are motivational differences in respect to putting the Law into practice.

Jesus begins by stating the general principle of the decalogue: "You shall not kill, you shall not bear false witness, etc." He then proceeds to define the Law in all its radicality. Not only anger, but insult and the unkind word will be punishable on the day of judgment. Adultery that proceeds from the thought, eye or hand may be subject to the fires of hell. Reconciliation with the accuser is counselled even on the way to the court for judgment. Relationships are key to the message of Jesus; above all with accusers or enemies. "To offer your gift at the altar if anyone has anything against you, will profit you nothing." The message is clear and profoundly simple. In applying Jesus' message to the Jewish Christian community, Matthew encourages them to make the Golden Rule integral to all their relationships and to relate to all other persons as themselves. For the Jews and the Gentiles who saw themselves as distinct and separate from each other, this must have been exceedingly difficult.

The climax of Chapter 5 deals with the relationship with our neighbor: do not retaliate or be revengeful. The teaching on relationships advocates that we love even our enemy and pray for those who persecute us because we are all children of the one God. God in heaven allows the sun and the rain to be lavished upon the evil and the good, the just and the unjust (Matt 5:45). God shows the same "face" towards all. There are two options: to love those who love us, which is human; or to love even our enemies; which is God-like. What Jesus upheld and taught as the spiritual norm of human life is the ultimate paradox: "Be perfect as your heavenly Father is perfect" (Matt 5:48).

Perfect is derived from the Greek word *teleios*. It is a process word, an adverb or action word. When it is applied to God, it indicates that God is always acting from the point of view of the END; that which is completed. God is in the process of bringing about the time of the END since God's will is to be with us here and hereafter. *Perfect,* when applied to the teaching of the Sermon on the Mount, advocates that all actions be fully one with God who is GOOD and who acts from the perspective of the END. Jesus is the perfect human person, the JUST ONE (Matt 27:21) who has most fully attained the glory-image in obedience to the will of God. He has achieved the goal to be where God is! Jesus has attained the end-time fulfillment. Jesus embodies the completion of God's promise and God's purpose: to be "God-with-us" (Matt 1:23) and to remain with us (Matt 28:20). Jesus is the way to the goal where God is. To be in the process of perfecting our choices for GOOD/GOD, truth/justice will be evident in what we do and teach. "Say 'Yes' or 'No' to God; more than this is said out of evil" (Matt 5:37).

Be Perfect

TWO WAYS OF PRACTICING JUSTICE (Matt 19:16-21)

The story of the rich young man provides valuable insight into the normative value of justice in praxis. The question of the rich young man is a timeless one; it is the quest of every person who seeks purpose and meaning in life: "Teacher! What good deed must I do to enter into eternal life?" (Matt 19:16).

Jesus responds with a counterquestion and a corrective that penetrates even to the mind and heart of human experience.

"Why do you ask me concerning the good? ONE is GOOD! If you wish to enter into life; keep the commandments" (Matt 19:17). Jesus makes no distinction between good and God; between life and eternal life. This is God-like. Enter into the presence of the Good-God, and you will enter into life now and eternally, for God is the one existing reality.

The mandate to keep the commandments provokes another question: "What specific commandments must I observe in order to enter into life?" The commandments are the very basic, simple laws of nature, the code of life written on the human heart. They are the ageless, clear and concrete teachings: "Do not kill. Do not commit adultery. Do not steal, Do not bear false witness. Honor your father and your mother." All these are summed up in the command: "Love your neighbor as yourself" (Matt 19:18f). Therefore, the way to enter into life with God *now* involves a relationship with our neighbor.

Since the commandments reside in the heart of every human being, they are incumbent on every person in this world. In spite of the Law's specificity for Jewish practice, the law of justice is universal; peoples of every culture, religion, political or social persuasion are bound by it and seek it. The commandments are a reflection of the universal law of justice and provide insight into the value that God gives to the human person and to life in this world. To respect and love the other person as oneself is both divine and human. Observance of the commandments indicates a perception of life that leads to a vision of the fullness of life and love here and hereafter.

The restlessness engendered, the incompleteness that is felt in the rich young man due to the limitless desires of the mind, heart and spirit, prompt him to probe more deeply. The commandments are not sufficient. He requests the one thing that is still lacking. Jesus responds, "If you will be perfect: go sell all that you possess, give to the poor and you shall have treasure in heaven; and come follow me!" (Matt 19:21). Life here and now is eternal life begun. It is a process of living out the goal of the end-time and realizing the presence of "God-with-us." This process requires a decision and an action on our part that flow from the fundamental choice we have made to bear the name Christian through baptism (Matt 28:19; 3:6). Jesus himself reveals to us what it means to be fully human, and what it means to be believer. "Come, follow me!" (Matt 19:21).

TWO WAYS OF ENTERING THE KINGDOM

The Sermon on the Mount gives us new insight into the presence of God or the kingdom of heaven: God is present when the Law is observed. Justice according to the Law follows scribal teaching (Matt 5), fulfills religious duties (Matt 6), moral demands and juridical stipulations (Matt 7). But the Law, as practiced in Judaism, is comprised of many requirements over and above the core of Wisdom's teaching: ". . . do to others as you would have them do to you" (Matt 7:12).

Faith in the presence of "God-with-us" in the END-TIME effects a change of mind and heart that allows us to perceive the kingdom of heaven at hand. If we seek God's kingdom and justice first, God's will for the *good* and the *true*, then it will be possible to choose the presence of God in the midst of false gods, the idols, the requests for the things we think we need that are less than GOD and obscure God's gift of life. It is possible for us to fill our minds and hearts with idols. When walls of desire begin to imprison us, we are unable to grasp the revelation of God that Jesus has given us in his incarnate being.

The Jesus of Matthew's Gospel tells us that whatever we do in faith is done for God in the person of the other. The Jesus of Matthew's Gospel also tells us to do nothing other than deal with the other person as ourselves. This fulfills all justice on a personal, national and international level.

This is the key to the entire Sermon on the Mount that stands as climax and conclusion: "Whatsoever you wish that others do to you, do to them, for this is the Law and the Prophets" (Matt 7:12). This is justice and this is wisdom built on the foundation of the teachings of Jesus: "Be perfect as your heavenly Father is perfect" (Matt 5:48).

The message of Jesus is universally freeing. Matthew's genius was to realize the implications of that teaching for both Jews and Gentiles; namely, to free and accept the other as themselves. God's liberality encompasses vastly diverse points of view. This is an astounding fact. To free the other person from our expectations and judgment is to give life to the other and to do good. This is the challenge and responsibility of a lifetime. It is also the challenge and responsibility of the Church as it endeavors to reconstitute the community today. The Church community, like the individual, faces the same tension and experiences the same ambivalence that confronted the first hearers of the Sermon on the Mount.

The instructions of Jesus in the Sermon on the Mount are the least of the commandments but they invite everyone into the realm of the kingdom. "If you relax one of these least commandments and teach others to do so you will be called least in the kingdom of heaven. If you do and teach them you will be called great in the kingdom of heaven" (Matt 5:19). The kingdom of heaven includes the little ones and the great. And the least of the commandments carries an interior dimension that touches and involves even our thoughts and desires.

Matthew's message to his divided community is a compendium of God's word to Jeremiah in exile. It is a compendium of
Jesus' word and a prophetic message for today:

> "But this is the covenant which I will make with the house of
> Israel AFTER THOSE DAYS, says the Lord: I will put my law
> within them, and I will write it upon their hearts; and I will be
> their God, and they shall be my people. And no longer will each
> one teach his/her neighbor and his/her brother and sister,
> saying: 'Know the Lord,' for they shall all know me, from the
> *least* of them to the *greatest,* says the Lord; for I will forgive their
> iniquity and will remember their sin no more."
>
> (Jer 31:33f.)

4

Presence:
The Fulfillment of the Wisdom of God
on Behalf of the Kingdom

Wisdom

What precisely is God's Wisdom that describes the spiritual "WAY" for Matthew's community of believers? Wisdom is difficult to define, but Matthew's Gospel portrays the person of Jesus as Wisdom Incarnate and depicts his function as Wisdom Teacher for the Christian community of Jews and Gentiles alike.

By adeptly combining the universal images of Wisdom with the revelation of God's Law, Matthew offers the Jewish-Christian community a Wisdom Christology. It is the aim of the one who formulates a Christology to portray the Christ in a way that relates to life so that Jesus may remain present and active in the community. This continuing presence of Jesus as WISDOM remains traditionally faithful to the message of God's saving LOVE and also becomes universally meaningful in Matthew's Gospel.

In order to appreciate fully Matthew's genius as a theologian and a spiritual writer, some background may be helpful before considering the school of Wisdom teaching.

ISRAEL AND THE ANCIENT NEAR EAST

In an Ancient Near Eastern environment, the term wisdom specifies a form of folk literature that embodies thoughts concerning life gained by practical human experience. These popular rhythmic sayings pass from person to person expressing observations that are common, ordinary and acknowledged to be true by many peoples. As such, wisdom is a form of thinking common to humankind. It is a particular form of intellectual activity, although it is not intellectual knowledge. It is a form of knowledge that is reasonable and engaging; it engages one in the search for an abundance of life.

One of Wisdom's main objectives is directed toward assessing right relationships in life. Wisdom's perceptions recognize a certain order and harmony at work in the universe. Based on what is seen and heard in the realm of this world, wisdom concludes that nature has its own inbuilt laws. Consequently, wisdom's field of knowledge or thought encompasses the vast arena of the world: one knows what to expect in life and what to expect from life. Therefore, expectations become an activity that involve the whole of one's life from beginning to end. If one waits with patience it will surely come about! Even though there are different facets to one's personal life such as managing the household, one's body and even the tongue (cf. Prov 12:18f; 15:2, 4), wisdom concludes that the laws that pertain to the physical realm also circumscribe the political, social, educational and the religious realms.

As a result analogies abound in wisdom speech and wisdom's perception of reality. Comparisons are made between different orders of reality using patterned sayings:

> "Four things on earth are small,
>   but they are exceedingly wise;
> the ants are a people not strong,
>   yet they provide their food in the summer;
> the badgers are a people not mighty,
>   yet they make their homes in the rocks;
> the locusts have no king,
>   yet all of them march in rank;
> the lizard you can take in your hands,
>   yet it is in kings' palaces."
>
> (Prov 30:24-28)

There is a concentrated list of metaphorical expressions co-ordinated with "like" or "as":

> "I will again make instruction shine forth like the dawn
>   and I will make it shine afar;
> I will again pour out teaching like prophecy,
>   and leave it to all future generations,
> Observe that I have not labored for myself alone,
>   but for all who seek instruction":
>
> (Sir 24:32-34)

Throughout the proverbial sayings, contrasting situations are highlighted by means of the repetitious "but" or "better than":

> "The memory of the righteous is a blessing,
>   but the name of the wicked will rot."
>
> (Prov 10:7)
>
> "It is better to be of a lowly spirit with the poor
>   than to divide the spoil with the proud.
> The one who gives heed to the word will prosper,
>   and happy is the one who trusts in the Lord."
>
> (Prov 16:19)

These challenging statements are attempts to bring peoples' knowledge of life and its meaning into harmony and relationship with the well-governed, well-ordered universe.

Wisdom accomplishes this task by means of reason. Rooted in reason, planted on the soil of human experience, wisdom grows and prospers on sound, common judgments. "If one sows injustice, one will reap injustice" (Prov 22:8). The one who lives in order and harmony respecting the rightful claims of others (especially the poor) will live justly (Prov 29:7). In the language of wisdom, this person is called righteous; this is the "way" of wisdom (Prov 4:10-19). To obtain wisdom is to gain insight (Prov 4:1, 5, 7); therefore, it is better that one aspire and seek wisdom, than rely on one's own wisdom (Prov 3:5), indicating that the divine, transcendent quality of wisdom is to be sought. "Say to wisdom, you are my sister, and call insight your intimate friend" (Prov 17:4).

Surprisingly, a divine norm is not mentioned in the wisdom literature of the rest of the Ancient Near East. And it is readily seen from the poetic teachings documented by the Book of Proverbs that the Wisdom literature of Israel is not unlike that of the Ancient Near East. Israel has adapted the wisdom sayings as an educational form of instruction mainly because proverbial sayings are indigenous to all nations and cultures. At heart, all peoples inquire and seek, or engage in the perceptive search for what we commonly call wisdom.

WISDOM IN EXILE

It is not surprising, however, to discover that the persuasive power of Israelite wisdom lay not in human reason alone, but in its verification by the Law. After Israel's deportation into

Babylon, the land of Exile, in 587 B.C., prophecy and kingdom slowly declined. Israel was thrown back upon the Law as the sole means to know and understand the Will of God. Israel's way of life in this world, guided and directed by the Word of God, issued from the divine commands or the Law. No longer was the prophet able to remind the people Israel of its covenant relationship; no longer was the royal kingdom or the magnificent Solomonic temple the place where comparisons with other nations were to be made. It was in the unconventional mingling and contact with the Egyptian and Babylonian nations, alienated and separated from the homeland, that Israel was instructed by the Deuteronomist:

> "I have taught you statutes and ordinances as the Lord my God commanded me, that you should *do* them in the land which you are entering to take possession of it. Keep them and *do* them; for that will be your WISDOM and UNDERSTANDING in the sight of the peoples, who when they hear all these statutes, will say, 'Surely this great nation is a *wise* and *understanding* people.' For what great nation is there that has a god so near to it as the Lord our God is to us, whenever we call upon God? And what great nation is there, that has statutes and ordinances so righteous as all this *Law* which I set before you this day?"
>
> (Dt 4:5-8)

But the message continues:

> "Only take heed, and keep your soul diligently, lest you forget the things which your eyes have seen and lest they depart from your heart all the days of your life; make them known to your children and your children's children . . ."
>
> (Dt 4:9)

Small wonder then that for Israel the Law was designated the wise and the ultimate means to know and understand the Will of God. Therefore, when the temple and the land were destroyed, the people of God were instructed by the prophets to look to the covenant renewal in the heart for security and consolation (Jer 31:31ff; Ezek 33:34). When prophecy ceased, only then did Israel turn to the Wisdom writers whose ultimate aim, consistent with these prophetic reminders, was to maintain right order and just relationships.

WISDOM IN TRANSITION

The body of Wisdom literature that parallels the Law and the Prophets in the Books of the Old Testament, has as its main theme Wisdom as found in God. This Wisdom remains with God but also proceeds from God and enters into humankind (Prov 8:32ff). Solomon, the most famous proponent of God's gift of Wisdom in Israel, sought to know and to understand wisdom so that he might judge the people rightly (1 Kgs 3:7-12). As king of Israel, Solomon's reputation as the incomparable sage was enhanced and the people themselves were esteemed highly by all the nations in the then-known world. Israel could truthfully say: "No other nation has its god *so near* to it as *our God is to us* whenever we call" (Dt 4:7).

In Israel's earliest Wisdom writings, wisdom is not personified. However, in Sirach, written during the second century B.C., Wisdom (Sophia, feminine) speaks in the first person, presenting herself as the Law:

> ". . .rooted in an honored people, who receive the Lord's inheritance (Sir 24:12), the tree grew tall with *abundant fruit* (Sir 24:13, 15, 17). Wisdom invited 'Come to me, you who

desire me, and eat your fill of my produce (Sir 24:19). . . . *those who eat me will hunger for more, and those who drink me will thirst for more.* Whoever obeys me will not be put to shame and those who work with my help will not sin' (Sir 24:21f). All this is the book of the covenant of the Most High God, the Law which Moses commanded us as an inheritance for the congregation of Jacob. It (the Law) fills persons with wisdom" (Sir 24:23, 25).

Wisdom's perceptions of the eternal truths of nature, as well as the Law revealed by God, are considered to be manifestations of Divine Wisdom. "All wisdom is from God" (Sir 1:1). And since the Law and Wisdom are both manifestations of Divine Wisdom, the Law eventually becomes identified with WISDOM. It goes forth from God as Word and enters into persons, giving wisdom a personality of her own. Thus, the Law is a concretization of the Wisdom of God and it follows that the observance of the Mosaic Law is a prominent element in relating to all nature's gifts. The objective order of nature as well as the subjective gift of personal wisdom is revelation and the place where God can be found.

Wisdom also has its practical side. There are ethical dimensions in wisdom's education. Practical wisdom teaches one to live rightly and consists in knowing how to live with discernment and insight. The wise person accepts God's Will as set forth in the Law. Fear of God is thus the beginning of wisdom (Prov 1:7; 9:10; 15:33; 30:3), and expresses devotion and piety that translates the relationship of God with the children of Israel into the fullness of wisdom (Sir 1:16). Fear of the Lord is also the root of wisdom (Sir 1:20) and the basis of all religious observance. Therefore, the one who holds steadfastly to the Law will obtain wisdom (Sir 14:25; 15:2).

Another second century writing, entitled the Wisdom of Solomon, written on the soil of the Hellenistic world, describes

Wisdom personified as the builder and architect of *all* who continues to penetrate the hearts of *all* (Wis 7:24) entering in (Wis 7:27) and renewing *all things* (Wis 8:1). Although she fills the universe, she is a breath (a word) of the power of God as well as a reflection of the eternal light and an image of the Divine "Good" (Wis 7:25-27). Wisdom is not only universal law but also the universal "gift."

The wise person within the ranks of Judaism prays and petitions God:

> "Send forth wisdom from the throne of your greatness, that she may be with me and toil, and that I may learn what is pleasing to you. For she knows and understands all things and she will guide me wisely in my actions and guard me with her glory. Then my work will be acceptable and I shall judge your people justly."
>
> (Wis 9:9-12)

And the wise one continues with this acclamation:

> "Who would have learned your counsel, unless you had given WISDOM and sent your HOLY SPIRIT from on high? And thus the path of those on earth was set RIGHT, and persons were taught what pleases you and were saved by WISDOM."
>
> (Wis 9:17f)

This paraphrase of Solomon's prayer from I Kings 3:6-9 parallels the coming of the Holy Spirit, who informs the persons who bear the gift of Wisdom, so essential for discerning the proper and the righteous way of acting in accordance with the Law.

Wisdom and the Law have passed through all generations and ultimately Wisdom and the Law are subject to personification, incarnation and depiction according to the personality of the believers. God has expanded this gift of wisdom by giving *new life* to anyone who is able "to hear and to do" the Law as it is written in the heart of the human person. This is WISDOM. This is God-like, "Observe that I have not labored for myself alone, but for all who seek instruction" (Sir 24:34).

The universal dominion of wisdom was obviously of concern to Israel. Her preoccupation centered around separation from other peoples as a means of expressing her uniqueness. Wisdom had found a home in Jacob (Sir 24:8), but now a shift or change is apparently taking place within the community of the people of God.

At this juncture in Israel's history, a time of crisis and hopelessness, Wisdom appears as the ordainer of all human events as well as the designer of nature's marvels. Just as the Law becomes equated with Wisdom and conversely Wisdom becomes equated with Law, in first century Judaism, Wisdom becomes incarnate in Jesus, and Matthew's Jesus teaches God's Wisdom as Law.

No matter how we try to analyze or define her, Wisdom remains elusive. Yet it takes but a simple step to discover Jesus as the personal embodiment of the Wisdom of God incarnate in this world. Matthew attempts to unite the heavenly and the earthly realm of the kingdom of heaven on earth by the use of wisdom instruction. He not only succeeds but even excels in showing forth the unity of all peoples under God through the use of the Wisdom motif. In Jesus, the Wisdom Teacher, this new life of the divine and the human encounter is disclosed.

JESUS, THE WISDOM OF GOD

The Wisdom of God makes a final appeal through Jesus, the Incarnate One, who provides the *way* and the *place* for the decisive personal encounter between God and humankind. The Christ, as Wisdom, had a particular attraction for the specific Hellenistic Jewish Christianity which Matthew represents.

Matthew begins a collection of sayings of Jesus with a particular reference to the deeds of the Christ (Matt 11:2): "The blind receive their sight, the lame walk, lepers are cleansed . . ." (Matt 11:5-6 = Isa 35:5-8). Matthew concludes the teaching by quoting Jesus as saying, "Yet Wisdom is justified by her deeds" (Matt 11:19). The Christ, whose deeds were proclaimed abroad, scandalized the unbelieving hearers in whom the word did not take root (Matt 13:21, 57). The Pharisees, too, were scandalized by what they heard as a prophetic indictment of themselves: "This people honors me with their lips, but their heart is far from me; in vain do they worship me, teaching as doctrines the precepts of men" (Matt 15:8-9 = Isa 29:13). In a form of Wisdom speech, Jesus praised as BLESSED ". . .the ones who are not scandalized by me" (Matt 11:6). This association of the Christ with the prophetic word and the deeds of wisdom, clearly identifies Jesus as personified Wisdom.

In this same context, Matthew continues the presentation of the Good News in wisdom imagery: "This generation is like children sitting in the market places and calling to their playmates" (Matt 11:16; cf. Prov 1:20-22; Wis 8:1-4). The envoys of Wisdom, John and Jesus, offer differing ways of righteousness for their respective followers. Eating and drinking, as well as fasting and ascetical practices are the ordinary rituals of everyday life espoused by Wisdom (Matt 11:16-19; cf Sir 31-32). But because these practices had become law, "a precept of men" as it is stated in Matt 15:9, both John and Jesus were rejected by their own who could not agree on the forms of ritual observance. Given these unfortunate circumstances, Matthew is not satisfied merely to present Jesus as a messenger of Wisdom, alongside John. Matthew takes that additional step and identifies Jesus with Sophia herself:

> "Come to *me*, all you who labor and are heavy laden,
> and I will give you rest. Take *my* yoke upon you,
> and learn from *me;* for I am gentle and lowly in heart,
> and you will find rest for your souls. For *my* yoke
> is easy, and *my* burden is light."
>
> (Matt 11:28-30 = Sir 51:23-27)

These verses, specific to Matthew's Gospel, follow upon another Wisdom theme related to the mutual knowledge of the Father and the Son:

> "*All things* have been delivered to me by my Father;
> and no one knows the Son except the Father, and no
> one knows the Father except the Son and any one to
> whom the Son chooses to reveal him." (Matt 11:27)

Could this reciprocal knowledge of the Father and the Son be rooted in the Wisdom tradition that implies a unique and singular knowledge between God and Wisdom? "Only God knows Wisdom" (Sir 1:6, 8) and "only Wisdom knows God" (Wis 7:25-27). Wisdom lives with God, and God loves her. She knows God and is associated with God's works (cf. Wis 8:3ff). Wisdom was present at the creation of the world and Wisdom understands what is pleasing in the sight of God and what is right according to the commandments (cf. Wis 9:9).

God is the source, the locus of Wisdom; Wisdom is hidden and known only to God and found in Torah (Sir 24:23).

The *place* of Jesus as mediator of the knowledge of God as Father, and the *way* Jesus expressed the authoritative word of God that scandalized so many of his followers do not necessarily define the exclusivity of the Father-Son relationship as Wisdom. There is also the consideration that the community of Israel will be given the dominion and glory and kingdom over "all things . . ." in the apocalyptic age (Matt 11:25-27). This image refers to the Danielic figure of the Son of Man (Dan 7:14), a symbol of the people Israel, the elect, the chosen ones of Yahweh who will share in God's authority over all things in the end-time. This Father-son relationship of Israel to Yahweh is the special claim of the Jewish community.

With the claim that Jesus is as the righteous one (Matt 27:19 = cf. Wis 2:13, 16), the Son of God of the last days (Matt 3:15; 4:3, 6 = cf. Sir 4:10; 51:10), the mutual knowledge of Yahweh and Israel has come to fullest expression in the personal Word of God, Jesus, who assumes the authoritative WILL OF GOD in this *new age*. "Amen, I say to you . . ." and "You have heard it said, but I say to you . . ." (Matt 5:21-48) give God's Son the ultimate authority as well as the universal authority of God's Word/Wisdom/Torah. Jesus, the One faithful Israelite, represents the community of Israel in the last days.

The uniqueness of Matthew's insight comes to light where Jesus speaks as WISDOM. Jesus calls out and invites all pupils to take HIS YOKE upon their shoulders (Matt 11:28-30 = Sir 51:23-27). Jesus presents himself as Wisdom. Sirach had directed the students toward the future when this Wisdom would be realized by her children.

In one of the commissioning motifs, Matt 23:34-36, Jesus is

said to send prophets and wise men and scribes (Matt 23:34). This statement sums up the previous history of Israel as it is summed up in the Book of Wisdom, chapters ten and eleven. "Wisdom rescued the righteous" (Wis 10:9) and "prospered the works of Israel by the hand of a holy prophet" (Wis 11:1); ". . . but you are merciful to *all* because you can do *all things*" (Wis 11:23; Wis 15:1). Jesus is said to be continually sending envoys—messengers to teach and baptize (Matt 28:19) in the ministry of preaching the Word and in defense of Christianity in the face of Rabbinic Judaism.

In another prophetic appeal and lament over Jerusalem, Jesus as the person of Wisdom speaks of gathering her children as a hen (Matt 23:37-39), the maternal image of Sir 1:15. Jesus, making a final appeal to the children of Israel, is rejected by the religious authorities centered in Jerusalem. The Christ, as the Son of Man, is to come again soon (Matt 10:23; 24:44). This apocalyptic image of the revelation of God to Israel, together with the image of Wisdom, developed the Christological emphasis of Matthew's Gospel. This emphasis is significant because Jesus is the final, end-time messenger of Wisdom. Jesus is the close intimate of God and the fullest embodiment of Divine revelation as Word/Wisdom/Torah.

WISDOM IN MATTHEW'S COMMUNITY

Jesus, the Wisdom of God, established the new order of creation. Wisdom's penetrating power is fulfilled now that God is present in Jesus (Matt 1:21-23). The apocalyptic symbol, the kingdom of heaven, best expressed Israel's expectations of God's Presence in this new age; DIVINE WISDOM, that speaks to all nations, best expressed the universal sovereignty of God who has not abandoned Israel nor the world.

Because of Jesus' birth, death, resurrection and exaltation to *new life,* the whole economy of God's Law has changed. In the present reality of the new age, wisdom, the law of the human heart, speaks to the believers of the Will of God. As children of Wisdom, the Law of God or the Spirit of Divine Love becomes incarnate in the Christian community.

But life is also a future reality because of the event of the death/resurrection that has changed forever the meaning and the purpose of human existence. For those who have grown up with the understanding of life after death, it is difficult to comprehend what it must have been like for the members of Matthew's community to hear the message that their Messiah and leader was crucified, died but is raised up and remains with them as "Wisdom."

A generation after the life, death and resurrection of Jesus, Matthew's community received this message in a different context. In the words of Jesus, Matthew informs the community that God is still with them (Matt 28:20). As Risen Lord, Jesus remains with them until the end of time through the continuation of the Word concerning Jesus—embodied as the Wisdom of God. This enables the believers to perceive life in this world in two ways: *new life* in the kingdom is a present and a future reality; *new life* in the kingdom has a divine and a human counterpart because the kingdom of heaven is present here on earth. Thus, the kingdom symbol serves many purposes.

The kingdom symbol speaks to the inquiries and to the expectations of the Jews but Wisdom also leads to the kingdom. However, wisdom also speaks to the inquiries and to the expectations of the Gentiles. Undoubtedly, Matthew's community is perplexed: Why can the Christian be so free in

.regard to the Word of divine revelation handed on in the traditions of the Law and the Prophets? How can the Christian community be so free to re-interpret the Law and the Prophetic word of divine judgment in a manner that seems to resemble the Wisdom interpretations of the Gentiles? What is right conduct and right judgment if not guided by the Law and the statutes set down by Moses for the people Israel? Matthew is able to confirm that Wisdom's modes of presence as Person (TEACHER) and the Law (WORD) are not in conflict with the goals of the kingdom. They are ONE in Jesus.

God's gift of Wisdom Incarnate in Matthew's Gospel provides the power that is given to decide and to choose the RIGHT and the JUST. And to *do* the right is essential to fulfill all righteousness, or the Law (Matt 3:15). Knowledge is not adequate! "Produce fruit that befits repentance" (Matt 3:8, 10). Wisdom literature stresses the importance to "Do good deeds that show forth a change of mind and heart" (Prov 20:11). Therefore, Matthew quotes Jesus as saying, "Wisdom is justified by her deeds" (Matt 11:19). This teaching of Jesus enables one to hear and to UNDERSTAND God's Will (Matt 13:18ff; 15:10). For Matthew's community, Jesus, the Teacher and Wisdom Incarnate, is the way to know the Law that resides within the human heart and to act upon it in relationship to God, by treating others as oneself.

Matthew assures the community that Jesus is the gift of the Holy Spirit from on High (Matt 1:21; 3:11; 12:28), the gift of God's Presence. Baptism confirms that this Spirit is speaking within (cf. Matt 10:20). To be saved by Jesus is to be saved by God's Wisdom, since Jesus witnesses to a way of living in relationship to the present which is future life already begun.

Matthew's message concerning *new life* given to all through Jesus proclaims the message of Wisdom as the "way of God" with humankind. The Way/Will of God is not known for certainty; it is believed in faith. The security that derives from faith resides with God, not in the Law; not in the word that is remembered, not in the deed that is performed nor in the ritual acts of worship. Security is in God, since faith has the ability to constitute us in the realm of both earth and heaven at the same time, and to identify with "the other" as children of the one family under God. God makes both heaven and earth ONE in those sometimes fleeting moments when Wisdom is able to perceive that all things and all moments in this realm have the potential to become the means of human encounters. This comes about through God's gift of *new life* shared in and through the resurrected life of Jesus.

The Wisdom Relationship

The idea of Wisdom has thus moved beyond the sphere of human reason and knowledge of the Law to personal relationships as found in the life of the Teacher, Jesus. Wisdom is not intended to be merely inspiration, a subject of instruction or a lesson to be learned. The wisdom of old taught that the fear of God and knowledge about God is the beginning of wisdom. However, these elements of fear and knowledge affect the process of perception rather than the content of the teachings. Not fear of God but love of and knowledge about God are at the core or center of wisdom's pedagogy, and faith is definitely a primary factor in wisdom's tutorial system. Wisdom impels the person to excel with regard to knowledge of the world and execution of right behavior towards others. Likewise, it is believed that wisdom, informed by faith in Jesus, guides, protects and supports whoever seeks God and desires instruction. To do the right and the good, to treat the "other" as the "self" exemplify one's personal relationship with Jesus while adhering to wisdom's instruction (cf. Matt 7:12).

In Jesus' School of Wisdom, the wise person is not endowed with a certain amount of intellectual knowledge or acumen, nor even an abundance of practical skills. The wise person has a certain vibrancy or spirit of life which is attentive, alert, open "to hear and to do." The wise person has the capacity to learn and to be taught; is capable of receiving instruction and acting on it. The person who is wise is full of life and observes the nature of things, learns from these experiences and acts on them in dialogue with the sacred traditions (Matt 5:17-20).

In the eyes of the wise, the highest form of human existence is to listen, to reflect and to entrust oneself to the inner perception identified as wisdom. Therefore, when it comes to an understanding of reality, the wise person does not possess a kind of evidence that could satisfy everyone in every situation. Circumstances differ and different individuals perceive things differently through their inner eye of faith. Wisdom's way of thinking is always subject to doubts, fears and uncertainties, with the knowledge that one's personal perspective may not be shared by another.

Because this interior perception is verifiable only to the "self" and may not be in agreement with the "other," of necessity it places total reliance upon the "God" whom one does not see, yet believes; a God who is faithful, totally unpredictable but believed to be forever "with us." Perception made in spirit with the inner eye of faith is considered to be the judgment of the wise person. Although Jesus counsels one not to judge (cf. Matt 7:1), wisdom's judgment meted out in the realm of the spirit advocates merciful forgiveness and demands faith (Matt 23:23).Faith reflects on one's own perception, listens to the other's perceptions, and relies totally on God's perception. This trilogy of perceptions may not be in full agreement but wisdom's judgment is its highest acquisition, and wisdom's inner perception is, indeed, the highest form of human existence. A life of wisdom informed by faith in God, others, and self is a mode of contemporary theologizing, and acts as continuing revelation in today's world.

The beginning of wisdom is, therefore, the most sincere desire for instruction:

> ". . .and concern for instruction is love of her, and love of her is the keeping of her laws, and giving heed to her laws is assurance of immortality, and immortality brings one near to God; so the desire for wisdom leads to a *kingdom.*"
>
> (Wis 6:17-20)

The wise person also claims to have knowledge of God, and calls herself/himself a child of God and boasts of having God for Father (Wis 2:13, 16; Sir 4:10; 51:10). Wisdom calls this person a righteous Israelite, a disciple of wisdom. But this claim and more is applicable to Jesus. Jesus' own claim to a unique intimacy with his Father is implicit in his ministry and made certain in the innumerable instances where Jesus calls God "My Father" (Matt 6:9; 7:21; 8:21; 10:32; 11:27; 12:50; 15:13; 16:17, 27; 18:10, 14, 19, 35; 20:23; 25:34, 41; 26:29, 42).

Wisdom is a personal "way of life" that has implications for relationships in the communal "way of life" of the Christian community and in the world. Jesus testified to wisdom as the way of life of the community as opposed to the style of life of the Qumran community and the Jerusalem authorities. Jesus adds a new dimension to community life; the personal dimension of wisdom. Therefore, Jesus recommends the renewed interpretation of the Law of righteousness, traditional ritual observances and prophetic judgments in the light of Wisdom's personal Word/Way that fulfills the Law and the Prophets (Matt 5:20).

Jesus gives a new authoritative understanding concerning wisdom-righteousness in relationship to the scribal teachings: "You have heard it said . . . but I say to you" (Matt 5:21-48); wisdom-righteousness in relationship to Pharisaic teaching: "Beware of practicing your righteousness before the world in order to be seen . . ." (Matt 6:1-21); and wisdom-righteousness in respect to discipleship instruction: "With the judgment that you pronounce you will be judged . . ." (Matt 7:2). The antithetical Law statements, the pious practices of almsdeed, prayer and fasting as prescribed by the cult, and the ability to perceive and judge the will of God in the Sermon on the Mount, are all part of Wisdom's personal instruction (Matt 5-7).

As a communal way of life, wisdom assuredly gives life and allows for the life of the "other." For the Jewish Christian community, the principles and praxis of "the way of righteousness" relate to community life as legislated by the Law, covenant, ritual observances and judgments that fulfill the Old Testament prophetic cautions or warnings.

The persecution that the Jewish-Christian community was undergoing in Matthew's day was apparently a war centered on Law/Words (Matt 5:11). Slander, unjust accusations, defensive retaliatory speech are possibly attacks on the ways in which the synagogue and the church struggled to seek out and establish their identity. Matthew offers the Person of Jesus as Wisdom's personal "way of life" and Wisdom's way for the community of 85 A.D. He recommends that the disciples continually question their "way of life" while going towards the goal (Matt 5:48). Reserving judgment of good and evil until the final judgment day, and believing that the present situation of life is blessed and happy even now, is the goal of this *new life.* It is also Wisdom's way.

5

Presence:
A Spirituality for
the Christian Community

The Teaching of Wisdom

For Matthew the origin of the spiritual way of the Christian community begins with God's gift of WISDOM. In the *new age*, the Wisdom of God has become incarnate in Jesus. In other words, God has blessed the people with *new life* in and through Jesus and this is the beginning of a spirituality of PRESENCE.

Matthew opens the Sermon on the Mount with a litany of persons who are blessed, who hear and see Jesus and who are enabled to share Jesus' vision in the ordinary events of their daily lives. Matthew not only mentions the persons who are blessed now in the present circumstances, ". . .the poor in spirit; those persecuted for the sake of righteousness" (Matt 5:3, 10), but also the persons who possess and retain the gift of a future life with God, ". . .the mourners, the meek, those who hunger and thirst for righteousness, the merciful, the pure of heart and the peacemakers" (Matt 5:4-9).

These beatitudes sum up the Jewish-Gentile questions concerning *new life* in the kingdom. But the ninth beatitude also exposes the specific situation of Matthew's community of believers: "Blessed are *you* when you are subject to abusive language, persecuted and all kinds of evil is uttered against *you* falsely, on my account. Rejoice and be glad for your reward is great in heaven" (Matt 5:11f).

In the Sermon on the Mount, the Jesus of Matthew's Gospel urges the Christian community to superabound in the way of righteousness that they have received from the religious teachers within Judaism: "Unless your righteousness *exceed* that of the Scribes and the Pharisees, you shall not enter into the kingdom of heaven" (Matt 5:20). Righteousness which was implicit in the Law of Moses was made explicit in the words of the Prophets of former times. Now in the present *new age* the Law and the Prophets remain the underlying pre-requisite for the fulfillment of the right relationship with God and others. In fact, Jesus says: "I have come, not to abolish the Law and the Prophets but to fulfill them" (Matt 5:17).

At the same time, Jesus associates the Christian community of the *new age* with the prophetic stance of the old age. He suggests that, as Christians, whether Jew or Gentile, their prophetic task continues as hearers of the word of God. "Hear and do" but withhold judgment because God, as Law-giver, is judge and has reserved this prerogative of judgment for the end of time. Therefore "Do not judge and you shall not be judged . . ." (Matt 7:1).

Jesus continues to speak of the Law and the Prophets as expressive of the divine Love in the human condition and proposes a personal relationship which is lived in communion with God, others and self. Undoubtedly, the way of divine Love/Wisdom is the way of righteousness that continually transcends the ordinary way of life. The righteousness of the Jews and the Gentiles who were at enmity with one another over the question of their relationship to the teachings and observance of the Law and the Prophets is aptly expressed in the relationship of LOVE, even of enemies: "Love your enemies and pray for those who persecute you so that you may be children of your Father who is in heaven" (Matt 5:44). ". . . And if you greet your Jewish community members only, what more are you doing than others? Do not even the GENTILES do the same? (Matt 5:47). The Golden Rule, as it is often called, or the law of the Gentiles, is equally significant as a way of righteousness or the way of divine Love: "Whatever you wish that others do to you, do so to them . . . for this, too, fulfills the Law and the Prophets" (Matt 7:12).

It would seem that the Jesus of Matthew's Gospel stresses exceeding righteousness as the Law of divine Love but in a new context. God's Wisdom provides an equal opportunity for *all* peoples to hear the Law and the Prophets and to do justice. The unrestricted love prescribed for the Jews and the Gentiles also fulfills the two great commandments of love of God and of neighbor (friend/enemy) as the self. And Jesus maintains that all the while the Law and the Prophets may be summed up in the ONE LAW: LOVE. "You shall love the Lord your God with all your heart and all your soul, and with all your mind. This is the great and first commandment. The second is *like* it. You shall love your neighbor as yourself. On these two commandments depend *all* the Law and the Prophets" (Matt 22:37-40).

Matthew gives further insight into the way the Christian community is to superabound in righteousness. Throughout the Sermon on the Mount, Jesus warns the Jewish-Christian community about doing their righteous practices in the manner of hypocrites, in order to be seen by others. Whether it be almsdeed, prayer or fasting, the externals of the Law, such as rites and duties of worship are observable and usually are done in the company of others (Matt 6:1f, 5, 16). Therefore, they have received their reward. But Jesus advocates a manner of hiddenness where God who sees in secret will reward you in return (Matt 6:4, 6, 18). The danger of public worship is the enhancement of "the self" or even "the other" or the community making a public display of itself rather than entering into submissive service of God.

In another litany, this time of prophetic "woes," Jesus warns the Scribes and the Pharisees of the dangers of pretentious sacrificial ceremonies. It is easy to give to God from the superabundance of the earth's mint, dill and cummin. These sacrifices of material possessions and ritual observances are not to be scorned. But the weightier matters of the Law should not be neglected: *judgment* (translated JUSTICE in most instances), *mercy* and *faith* (cf. Matt 23:23). This is KEY to the anomalous Christian message that pleads for exceeding or superabundant righteousness as a "WAY" to the goal: "Unless your righteousness *exceeds* that of the Scribes and the Pharisees, you shall not enter into the kingdom of heaven" (Matt 5:20). It would appear that God's judgment, mercy and faith pave the way for transcending the traditional practices of TORAH righteousness. The sacrificial service of "the other," especially the persons in need, is the greater act of worship and means of reconciling God/self/other.

Undoubtedly, Matthew is concerned about the way of life within the Christian community. The life-style of the synagogue observers modeled Christianity on the Law. Jesus invites the crowds as well as his immediate followers into a relationship that is not judged by externals. The doing of the very least of the commandments, even ONE, the love of neighbor as the self, is adequate for participation in the way of life as a Christian (cf. Matt 22:39). In fact, "If you do and teach the least of these commandments you will be called great in the kingdom of heaven—and if you do not, you will be called least in the kingdom of heaven" (Matt 5:18).

In the Christian world where Jesus has passed through death to new life with God, Jesus' way exemplifies the way of Christian righteousness. God's Wisdom invites all to "hear and do" righteousness as WISDOM speaks and is heard within the trysting place of the human heart. In this *new age* of salvation, Wisdom's way necessitates listening and reflecting on the Word. Wisdom's insight or inspiration informs the observer of the meaning of the Law and acts as a guide for the *new life* with Christ. The new covenant resides in the human heart and it is here that human beings encounter God and grow in loving response to self/others. In the field of the listening heart where WISDOM resides, this new way of life requires discerning judgment.

Wisdom's thought proceeds from an inner hearing and reflection on the Word of God as revealed in the events of daily life. When thought and expression meet with the insight of God/Jesus, the fruits of righteousness are produced. Wisdom's practical way is also Matthew's way of expressing the manner of living by judgment, mercy and faith. This is the very experience of Jesus himself who lived the transforming process of the human condition.

And to conclude the Sermon on the Mount, Matthew cites Jesus as encouraging the blessed to build their house upon rock, not upon sand so that it will be able to withstand the winds and the rains of stormy times. "Everyone then who *hears* these words of mine and *does* them will be *like* the WISE MAN who built his HOUSE upon the rock . . ." (Matt 7:24). Is this not another of Matthew's divine metaphors that offers the follower of Jesus an opportunity to be *like* the WISE MAN: to be *like* JESUS?

For all who build on the Christian tradition, that rock symbolizes Yahweh (God), Christ (Jesus) or Peter. The symbol has stood out as a rock of scandal, a stumbling block at times; at other times, a solid foundation and rock of security for all within God's *house*. For Matthew, however, house-building is both a communal and a personal endeavor. The ecumenical *house* (the kingdom of this world constructed by God) and one's personal *house* (the house of wisdom built by Jesus on faith and God's merciful judgment) symbolize this mammoth architectural feat. It is difficult to ignore Matthew's use of the image of the HOUSE OF WISDOM comprising Jews and Gentiles in the kingdom of heaven on earth, a temporary HOME as God created it to be!

The only faithful, righteous one, Christ, as Wisdom Incarnate, gives light to *all* that are in the *house* (Matt 5:15f). The person of Wisdom also shines in the world for all to see and give glory to God. The foundation or *Rock* upon which the Christian builds this house as a personal and corporate enterprise recognizes Christ's life and way as the gift of WISDOM and this is BEATITUDE. Wisdom's gift allows one to question and to discern the "way" to enter the house and the family of the "other" just as Jesus has become incarnate in the house and the family of David and in the kingdom of this world. The way of Jesus, as God's WISDOM, models the relationship for all peoples who accept God's gift of LIFE/LOVE and WISDOM.

The Sermon on the Mount begins and ends, then, with the invitation to all the wise whom Wisdom literature of the Old Testament has frequently singled out as BLESSED or HAPPY. Accordingly, it is not difficult to hear in the structural design of Matthew's Gospel, a spirituality of PRESENCE where God is the architect and builder of the HOUSE OF WISDOM. The image of the *house* permeates the Gospel as a leitmotif situating the Christian community within the kingdom or PRESENCE where God's rule and reign remain "with us" forever. In a prophetic book written several centuries before Christ, one of Wisdom's children chants the praise of God: "O Israel, how great is *the house of God!* And how vast the territory that God possesses! It is great and has no bounds; it is high and immeasurable" (Bar 3:24).

The House of Wisdom

Several issues are basic to an understanding of Matthew's use of the *House of Wisdom* as an image of the spirituality of PRESENCE. The mission to the Gentiles was supposedly a point of contention in Matthew's day, since Jesus himself instructed the twelve: "Go nowhere among the Gentiles, and enter no town of the Samaritans, but go rather to the lost sheep of the house of Israel!" (Matt 10:5ff). How can we legitimate this movement beyond the borders of Israel?

Another concern involved the conceptual framework of a mixed community of believers. If the message of Jesus is addressed to the Gentiles as well as to the Jews at the time Matthew was writing, then it is necessary that the instruction be in a language and a form that speaks to the people of other religious backgrounds and other cultural values. Above all, it must relate to the traditions of the Jews and demonstrate the continuity of the Christian teaching with the historical beliefs of the people of Israel, otherwise the question is reasonable: Is Christianity in continuity with the ancestral faith or is Christianity a new religion?

A third issue addressed the actual socio-historical situation of the community of Matthew as spelled out in the so-called ninth beatitude in the Sermon on the Mount: "Blessed are you, when people revile you and persecute you . . .for so did they persecute the prophets who were before you" (Matt 5:11). Suffering was integral to the mission ministry of the person and the work of Jesus as well as a constituent element of the beginnings of Christianity. Indeed, religious persecution has been endemic to Israel's way of life from the beginning of her call as a people of God.

But what is the spiritual dimension that Matthew's *House of Wisdom* contributes to the message of God's PRESENCE? How does one assess the value and the importance of this universal encounter?

By choosing Wisdom as the means of binding Christianity to Judaism, Matthew is faithful to the traditions of Israel and to those of the Ancient Near East. First of all, the *House of Wisdom,* accommodates the universal mission of the Christian community: "Go! disciplize all nations . . ." (Matt 28:16-20), and presents a universal message that both Jews and Gentiles are able to hear and subsequently live in practice. *Wisdom* is a way of speaking about God to which all peoples can relate since all wisdom proceeds from God and seeks to understand *life.* Wisdom arises from the depth of the human heart and even catches an occasional glimpse of God's truth, life and light (Matt 5:13-15).

Matthew's choice of identifying Jesus as Wisdom TEACHER and MASTER of the House offers Christianity the continuity with Israel's past traditional teachers of the Law and the Prophets. Judaism finds solace and consolation in Wisdom for its present situation of bereavement and loss after the destruction of the Temple in 70 A.D. For these displaced persons,

Wisdom also provides a HOUSE or a place where all peoples may seek refuge and come to SERVE, for service is an aspect of worship. The wedding of the Gentiles with the house and the family of David is celebrated as a nuptial feast (Matt 22:2-14). Now in Jesus, God's Wisdom Incarnate, the whole world is invited and afforded the opportunity to be at home with the ONE GOD and to sit at the banquet table in the kingdom with Jesus. "Wisdom *mixes* her wine (a double entendre) and sets forth her table" (Wis 9:1). God's Wisdom and God's gift prepare the inside and outside of the *House of Wisdom* as the place or locus of the PRESENCE of God in Jesus.

> "Wisdom builds her house and says: 'Come eat
> of my bread and drink of the wine I have mixed.
> Leave simpleness and live and walk in the way
> of insight!"
>
> (Prov 9:4f)

HOUSE OF ISRAEL

Perhaps by concentrating on Wisdom literature of the Hellenistic era Matthew may be accused of giving undue emphasis to the Gentile world view. But even in the earliest accounts of the historical writings of Israel, Wisdom sayings circulated in their society. At the high point of the history of Israel, the Solomonic period of the kingdom, the popularity of wisdom images was at its peak.

Various categories of thought and levels of meanings were given to the kingdom of Israel as *house*. Israel constituted the house or the family of David from the inception of the kingdom. The *house* may be the actual palace of the king or a reigning kingdom or dynasty, a nation or a state, a social or religious organization or community. Any or all of these can constitute the kingdom or ruling *house*. In any event, kingdom connotes a *house* as well as a household or family that rules and bears a lineage.

As a dwelling or a residence, the *house* may be a simple room or a single chamber, a hall or congregational meeting place; it may even be a small plot of earth whose only door is the canopy of heaven. The *house* also enshrines a storehouse of treasured memories, practices and traditions. It shelters and preserves all that is valued and prized as one's cherished possessions, be they family customs, ritual celebrations, or sacred memorabilia such as relics and altars. Above all the *house* is the structure where family members, extended family members and relatives gather or reside. It is the place where the host/hostess offers the social amenities of gracious hospitality.

The *house* or family of God perpetuates the primary elements of kinship. Wherever persons go they take the "house" with them. This symbolizes the family history, the true stamp of character of the family name whose history is also enacted through it. The family bears the common insignia of the covenantal bond of union—the marriage relationship. In the *house* where the bridal couple takes up residence, God extends and rebuilds the household anew—as is evident in the writings of the prophets (Jer 31:28; 33:7; 42:10). And in the expression of the prophetic hope for a *new age*, the house of Judah and the house of Israel are to be restored or rebuilt by a mutual covenant with God now written on the human heart (Jer 31:31-34). In this instance, house-building is an apocalyptic and a messianic concept that will reach completion only when the Son of Man comes into his kingdom at the end of time (Matt 16:18, 28).

The *house* signifies above all, the place into which Yahweh has entered into a special relationship with the people Israel. The *House of Wisdom*, therefore, is the most normal and natural place to be at home with God. It is the place to enter into an intimate relationship with God by listening to God's Wisdom as it speaks of righteousness or moral relationships and right conduct that reside in and proceed from the law within the human heart.

All believers, Jews and Gentiles, members of the household of God have a role to play, and bear a relationship and responsibility to God. Accordingly, Jesus "knowing their thoughts, said to them, 'Every kingdom divided against itself is laid waste, and no city or *house* divided against itself will stand.' And if I cast out demons by Beelzebul, by whom do your children cast them out? Therefore they shall be your judges. But if it is by the SPIRIT OF GOD that I cast out demons, then the *kingdom of God* has come upon you" (Matt 12:25). In this text, the image of the household is used to exemplify a political, religious analysis of the consequences of disunity. If we rely only on self against satanic powers, the allegiance is divisive and destructive. In this passage also, the house, city and the kingdom denote the place where the ministry of Jesus and the Christian mission originates and flourishes. It is by means of persons and communities that God's Spirit of life is perpetuated in this world.

Israel's previous history announced "those days" when God's Presence and rule were to be realized in her midst. Therefore, in "that day" you shall seek and you shall find; you shall knock and it shall be opened (cf. Matt 7:7f). But Matthew seems to be reminding the community that the God of Israel is to be found also by those who did not seek, by a nation that did not call on My Name (cf. Isa 65:1). Therefore, the words of the Prophet Isaiah reverberate in their hearing:

> "Thus says the Lord God:
> Behold my servants shall eat,
>   but *you* shall be hungry;
> Behold, my servants shall drink,
>   but *you* shall be thirsty;
> Behold, my servants shall rejoice;
>   but *you* shall be put to shame.
> Behold, my servants shall sing for gladness of heart,
>   but *you* shall cry out for pain of heart and anguish of spirit.

> . . .his servants he will call by a different name.
> So that he who blesses himself in the land,
>   shall bless himself by the God of truth.
> And he who takes an oath in the land,
>   shall swear by the God of truth;
> Because the former troubles are forgotten
>   and are hid from my eyes."
>
> (Isa 65:13-16)

And once again Isaiah, the prophet with universal vision recalls "that day":

> "Thus says the Lord: Heaven is my throne and the earth is my footstool; what is the *house* you would build for me and what is the place of my rest? All these things my hand has made, so all these things are mine, says the Lord. But this is the ONE to whom I will look; the one that is humble and silent and who trembles at my word."
>
> (Isa 66:1-2)

Figuratively speaking, to tremble means to be fearful or to stand in awe of my word.

The vision of the prophet Obadiah, one of the last of the prophets, announces "that day" of the Lord as near: "For the day of the Lord is near upon all the nations. As you have done it shall be done to you, your deeds shall return on your own head. For as you have drunk upon my holy mountain all the nations round about shall drink" (Obd 1:15-16).

This image of the *House of Wisdom* enables Matthew to move from the symbol of kingdom as a particular community of persons called by God to witness to the PRESENCE, to the universal community where all are welcomed into the family of believers. The image of the *House of Wisdom* also provides movement from the kingdom of heaven to the kingdom on earth as the one realm permeated by God's PRESENCE,

WISDOM, SPIRIT AND LIFE. The image of the *House of Wisdom* creates the ambiance for the individual in the context of the community to make hourly decisions for life or death in this world which is the realm of the sacred. These decisions have meaning for the present and for the future life to come.

THE BEATITUDES

The beatitudes make known the arrival of the grand opening "DAY" of the HOUSE OF WISDOM. The repetitive staccato note "HAPPY" heralds the clarion call to a *new life* in this *new age*. The opportunity is present:

> "Blessed/happy are the poor in spirit, for theirs is
>   the kingdom of heaven.
> Blessed are those who mourn, for they shall be comforted.
> Blessed are the meek, for they shall inherit the earth.
> Blessed are those who hunger and thirst for righteousness,
>   for they shall be satisfied.
> Blessed are the merciful, for they shall obtain mercy.
> Blessed are the pure of heart, for they shall see God.
> Blessed are the peacemakers, for they shall be called children
>   of God.
> Blessed are those who are persecuted for righteousness' sake,
>   for theirs is the kingdom of heaven.
> Blessed are *you* when men revile *you* and persecute *you* and utter
> all kinds of evil against *you* falsely on my account. Rejoice and be
> glad for *your* reward is great in heaven, for so men persecuted the
> prophets who were before *you*."
>
> (Matt 5:3-12)

The Teacher and the Master of the *house* announces that anyone from any position or status in life is called and challenged by these new perceptions of the reality of the kingdom on this earth. The world no longer poses a threat to one's existence. The forces or powers of the realm of evil no longer constitute a threat to a healthy, vibrant and integrated way of life. The world is the home of the *House of Wisdom*, the place of security and the place of vision where one is able to see, understand and know how God acts and how God discerns and judges. Jesus, WISDOM INCARNATE, is the rock, the foundation to believe that this world provides the place of the PRESENCE OF GOD where one can reside confidently in this WISDOM. The beatitudes signal the person and the world as the *house*, the shelter and the domain where God is to be FOUND.

The Greek word MAKARIOS may be translated blessed or happy; the meaning is basically the same. The beatitudes refer to persons whom God judges to be blessed/happy. God has blessed everyone with life and the gift of life communicates happiness for those who receive it. Happiness blossoms into the fullness of life in a goal-oriented existence that strives to live with God here and hereafter. The beatitudinal person possesses the eyes of faith to see, and the wisdom to hear and reflect on the situations in life in order to act rightly and extend God's merciful love without judgment. Beatitudes enable persons to build their relationships on inner happiness as a fact of life.

The beatitudes follow the classic teachings of the Law and the Prophets and the format of the Wisdom sayings. What the commandments presented as right and just was judged worthy of reward or punishment, blessing or curse by the prophets. But what is novel in Jesus' version of the beatitudes is the fact that these prophetic situations, normally cited as the occasion for God's judgment, now can become opportunities for limitless happiness. To be poor in spirit, mourners, meek, hungry and thirsty are situations of lack, destitution, want and suffering. It is against social conditions of injustice such as these that the prophets railed. But these occasions, normally condemned by the Pharisaic traditons of the Law, are now singled out as the precise occasions for the individual person to make a wise decision that will work for, not against the "self"; one can choose to exercise God's gift of merciful love toward the "other."

Is it possible to see and respond to God's unparalleled judgment in these situations of poverty, meekness, hunger and thirst for righteousness? The exceeding righteousness that Jesus speaks about is limitless and measureless. To observe the world through the eyes of faith requires a good to be done that is described in infinite terms. To be pure of heart, to be merciful, to be peacemakers and to suffer persecution, force one to go beyond the limits of the human to the divine. It takes the courage of unshakeable wisdom to break into the realm of peoples' lives, houses, cities and securities and lovingly tend to the needs of the "other" as family, whomever they may be. Wisdom bears this burden of the human and the yoke can become light since there is no external law that specifies how heavy the burden or how many duties one needs to perform. Jesus imposes no parameters on beatitudinal happiness. Wisdom discerns the exceeding righteousness, the limitless contribution that one can make because of God's gift of *new life* through death; the beatitudinal opportunities that confront one each day are innumerable.

Enticed by the catchword "blessed/happy," a form of wisdom speech, one looks hard to find negative or positive commands in these explicit personifications of wisdom-happiness. Free from specifics, the beatitudes allow one to formulate options regarding who are the poor in spirit, the mourners, and the meek. There is no way one can discern these interior conditions of persons by observing the Law. Every person is endowed with the wisdom to choose this blessed gift from God as the way to render service to and express love of the "other." It is the most human of acts to realize and recognize our bondedness as human beings in the realm of our human nature.

Jesus is speaking to a community that is known for its identification with the poor. The Qumran group of believers sought refuge in the desert and lived a communal existence identifying themselves as the "Community of the Poor." Would Matthew be addressing this situation of believers to counteract the community's expectations? Jesus had not come to institute a new religion but to instruct the community of people of God concerning God's way of life and Wisdom's perception of kingdom expectations.

The thought that poverty would vanish in the *new age* was common in first century Judaism and is a concept that has remained with us until this very day. Efforts to root out all situations and forms of poverty, sociologically, economically, religiously, and politically, look to Matthew's Sermon on the Mount, specifically the beatitudes, to justify their teaching and denunciation of poverty.

Matthew, however, puts a modifier to this beatitude and specifically reminds the community that God recognizes as HAPPY those who are poor *in spirit.* Matthew does not presume to make a modern dichotomy between the interior attitude of heart and exterior ethical behavior. Nor does Matthew presume to think that concern and help for the poor is peripheral or extraneous. This would not be the viewpoint of biblical peoples. Jesus provides the ultimatum: anyone who wishes to come after me must relinquish all rights to worldly gains and

provide for the poor with money procured by lawful means
(Matt 19:21). Yet, at the Last Supper, Jesus remarks: "You
have the poor with you always, but me you do not have
always" (Matt 26:9, 11). Thus, in the Christian era, the
mission is to preach the Good News to the poor (Matt 11:5)
and everyone who recognizes and responds to this need in the
"self" and the "other," will be ushered into the kingdom
(PRESENCE) of God (cf Matt 11:5). Who then are the poor in
Matthew's Gospel?

The poor in Matthew's day would presumably be the ones
whom Wisdom would identify as the untutored, the Gentiles
who are outside the Law and the ones who have not been
fortunate enough to be able to provide for themselves from the
land and the family of Israel. The ones who cannot gain
entrance into the community of the peoples of God mourn
because they are not of the land—the temple is destroyed and
the city itself is now in ruins. Food and drink, symbols of the
prophetic WORD and the LAW, are yet to be heard by and
dispensed to those who hunger and thirst for the rights and the
peace of others. In the teachings of Wisdom, "the other" as
"the self" is the ONE LAW and the ONE LOVE that Jesus
advocates for the children of God and the new way to
experience and FIND GOD (the kingdom of heaven on earth).

Perception and discernment are wisdom's WAY to reveal
outwardly what is seen/heard inwardly. Wisdom's perception
allows every person and thing in life to be surrounded and
affected by the beatitudinal gift. Uniting with the experiences
of "the other" and sharing one's own heart by extending
unshakeable support for those in a situation of LOSS provide
happiness—that exceeding righteousness—prescribed by the
LAW/LOVE.

To discern with wisdom, what will offer the fullest "life"

and "love," the most happiness in life, is the purpose of the beatitudes. To hear the call as the "happiness" that awaits fulfillment in anyone who chooses the right and the good for "the self' personally, so that "the self" can be identified with "the other," is to choose and meld with the Will of God. This was Jesus' own path and road and way to the goal. He did not see it imposed on him but freely accepted God's Will and chose it for himself. It was his response and his commitment to LOVE. And that, in every and all circumstances of life, is BEATITUDE. Therefore, the teachings of the beatitudes are deeply personal commitments to hearing the message of wisdom; seeking and finding the options open to us that will reveal or make known the Presence of God. The beatitudes allow God's Love to be experienced by all—only a limited horizon would prevent love from reigning (raining) on the just and the unjust, the evil and the good (cf. Matt 5:45).

The fruit of happiness is the product of one's decisions to act with mercy and compassion. Personal decisions and actions will fructify and grow in the rich soil and climate of love. The decisions we make are not only effective in directing our lives here in this world but also affect the life that lies ahead. These decisions are made in communion with God, and in the process of discernment they become creative acts. They bear more and more life to "the other" and to "the self." Good is thereby discovered as the treasure in the field or the pearl of great price (cf. Matt 13:44, 46). Seek and you shall find God/Good (cf. Matt 7:7; 19:17).

The old teaching of the Law and the new teaching of Wisdom both have as their highest norm, the supreme value of the human person. "The householder brings out of his treasure what is *new* and what is *old*" (Matt 13:52). By offering Wisdom's personal dimension to traditional teaching, is it not possible that Jesus is offering each person the option to grow in exceeding righteousness by permitting and encouraging personal discernment within the society or community? In an age of community consciousness, when the people of God depended upon the structures of their religion for their identity, was Jesus not calling them personally to a new type of justice and equality for all? Jesus calls each person to Wisdom's conduct that is mutually acceptable to the morality of the Jews and the Gentiles. Is it not possible that Wisdom's new "way" of righteousness will enable all peoples to live in tranquility and peace, love and order, and satisfy everyone for all time?

A way of life that shows deep moral concern for all persons is the focus of Jesus' message. The beatitudes do not center on systems that are prejudiced with regard to material or even spiritual inequalities in the community or in society. Jesus himself cares for all, the rich and the poor, male and female, the birds of the air as well as the lilies of the fields (cf. Matt 6:25-34). In an age when the externals of the Law paid a very high premium, how did Matthew's community receive and assess the value Jesus placed on the interior spirit? In Wisdom's inner exchange with God, self and the other, is it possible to touch the heart of "the other" as well as reach the mind and the heart of God? Is it possible not to see, but to believe that there is value in the hidden depth and the remotest corner of the mind and heart of the "other?" Can "the self" see and judge the need for a change in the "other"—whether it be moral, social, economic—and really know how to effect these changes for the good of the individual and/or the community?

To live by faith, to exercise mercy and trust in "the other," to withhold judgment on the purpose and meaning of life until the end, is the way of happiness, the way of Wisdom. When the judgment comes round at the end, it will be a judgment that rests on the hospitality that we have displayed in our homes, in our hearts and in our lives. It will depend on the feeding and the clothing and the visiting and the happiness that we have shared in this world in order to be welcomed into the eternal home and family of God (Matt 25:31-46). This is Wisdom's personal challenge and the personal responsibility of the wise to see, judge and act with merciful love (cf. Matt 23:23).

Jesus makes it clear in the beatitudes that right here and now opportunities exist for mercy and peace and vision as children of the ONE Father (GOD). And this beatitude/ happiness continues in the love that is extended personally to anyone who is willing to walk side-by-side and identify with "the other." This is the happiness of kingdom existence now and in the life to come. It identifies Matthew's beatitudinal spirituality.

Wisdom thinking, therefore, is capable of coordinating the incomprehensible, illusive nature of the divine with the human. This discerning thought process that occupies one's whole life, is common to humanity and concerns itself with every aspect of the human condition. Wisdom has found a home in the earthly soil of the created world in the individual's personal life.

For the readers of Matthew's day who were rooted in the Jewish tradition of TORAH, righteousness was more than interaction or casual relationships on a social level. According to the new interpretation of TORAH, right relationships were, indeed, sacred intra-world encounters. The Christian, at the deepest level of interdependence (in spirit) was encouraged to reverence God in the realm of all creation and preserve the relationship, balance and harmony within all of nature as ordered and ordained by God.

If the beatitudes are taken out of the context of Matthew's Gospel or the Sermon on the Mount, they may become objectives to be achieved or characteristics of life to be emulated or even demanded. However, those who recognize by faith God's gift of life in the human condition, possess the Wisdom of God and they are blessed/happy. They behold the face of God—the vision of God in "the other." God is found and experienced in relationship with "the other," even the enemy. The person who lives by faith makes no distinction. In God there is ONE LIFE, there is ONE LOVE, there is ONE SPIRIT, and there is ONE TRUTH—WHO IS WISDOM, extended to all. The search for the unknown in the known constitutes beatitudinal spirituality in Matthew's Wisdom Christology.

FAITH OF THE HOUSEHOLD

The *House of Wisdom* encompasses the many generations of believers in Israel: fourteen generations from Abraham to David, fourteen generations from David to the Exile, and fourteen generations from Babylon to Christ who is the fulfillment of this present time when God becomes one "with" us in Jesus (Matt 1:1-17). The present generation of believers in Jesus has the assurance that the Risen Lord, as Wisdom, will remain with them until the end of the age (Matt 28:20).

All the inheritors of the House of Israel participate in God's Wisdom and faithfulness especially in the present generation where they are blessed to see and to hear Jesus. "Truly, I say to you, many prophets and righteous ones longed to see what you see and did not see it and to hear what you hear, and did not hear it" (Matt 13:17). But there are those in Matthew's community designated "this generation" who have chosen not to see and not to hear and have rejected Wisdom Incarnate

(Matt 11:16-19; 12:39-45; 15:4; 23:34-39). Through unbelief and perversion of heart, the words of authoritative Wisdom become predictive: "Your house shall be left to you desolate" (Matt 17:17). But all will be gathered together in the end-time and then "this generation" will face judgment, the faithful and the unfaithful (Matt 24:34). "Heaven and earth will pass away but my words will not pass away" (Matt 24:35).

For entrance into the family and the household of Wisdom, God provides faith in Jesus as the door-way for all peoples. "Ask and it shall be given to you; seek and you shall find; knock and it shall be opened to you. For *everyone* who asks receives, and *everyone* who seeks finds and for *everyone* who knocks, the door shall be opened" (Matt 7:7-8).

The household includes the Gentiles, considered as the "other," who ask Jesus to enter into a relationship with them and yet find their personal *house* unworthy and hesitate to welcome (the Lord) under their roof (cf. Matt 8:8-10). There are the Jews who may be blind when they ask, seek and enter into the house of their own Son of David and brother. But Wisdom opens their eyes of faith to see JESUS (Matt 9:28-29). The vicarious faith of the Canaanite woman who approaches the Son of David in behalf of her daughter; the vicarious faith of the community who approaches Jesus in behalf of a paralyzed member-son; the woman who is made whole because she is bold in expressing her faith in Jesus; all have the inner perception to see and be restored to peace or the fullness of life (Matt 9:2, 22; 15:28). The people who follow Jesus at a distance are praised for their great faith, whereas the intimate disciples of Jesus are counselled concerning their "little faith" (Matt 17:20). But if one has faith even as the mustard, the smallest of seeds, the impossible becomes possible; if only one asks (Matt 21:21-22).

To ask with faith in a situation of being lost or experiencing loss of one's "self" in life creates the moment when a person can be found by Wisdom. Whether Gentile of Jew, male or female, individual or community, faith in Jesus' word as God's Wisdom Incarnate welcomes all into the House of God; all who enter into this *new life*, keep the commandment (Matt 19:17) and love the neighbor as "the self" (Matt 19:18; 7:14). But one is reminded that the gate is narrow that leads to this *new life* which presents a struggle and requires determination to enter.

NAME OF THE HOUSEHOLDER

In the Old Testament scriptures, "The Name" was a substitute expression for Yahweh. As a form of naming the divine, it signaled the Presence of God: "To make your Name dwell there" is the refrain that characterizes the building blocks of the Law in Deuteronomy (Dt 12:11, 21; 14:23f; 16:2, 11; 26:2). And since the traditions of Israel culminated in the Gospel writings, many of these linguistic forms serve to identify Jesus. Consequently, "The Name" had become one of those equative formulas for identifying Jesus as God.

"The Name" also identified the people of Israel who were considered to be the people who were "called by (your) Name" (Jer 7:10; 14:9, 30; Isa 43:7; 55:5f; Amos 9:12; Dan 9:19; Dt 28:10). Thus, the place where the Name dwelt was the all-encompassing element that constituted the place as a sanctuary. Whether it was a rock, an altar, a city or a mountain, the place of "The Name" was a Holy Place. And to further clarify the status of the divine and the human relationship, it is recorded in Dt 26:5, that Yahweh dwells in heaven but "The Name" dwells in the sanctuary on earth.

But not unlike "The Name," Wisdom personified is said to dwell in high places. She makes the circuit of heaven, walks in the depth of the abyss and on the waves of the sea: ". . . in *every people and nation* I have gotten a possession; among all these I sought a resting place; I sought in whose territory I might lodge" (cf. Sir 24:1, 5-7). In the manner of the divine, Wisdom comes to abide in the human, to participate in and dwell among the peoples of this earth. The "Name" becomes incarnate in Jesus and accomplishes God's saving deed in Israel.

Although the followers of Jesus in Matthew's community never receive a new name, as do the believers who were first called Christians in Antioch (Acts 11:26), it is through the significance of "The Name" [Jeshua, the Hebrew name for Jesus means salvation] that they receive forgiveness of sins (Matt 1:21) and function in the Name of Jesus as their Lord (Matt 7:22; 21:9; 23:39), as well as their Christ (Matt 24:5, 9). Merely invoking or calling upon the Name is not adequate for one to receive the empowerment and the authority of believers (Matt 7:21-23). To be worthy of Jesus, it is essential that one acknowledge Jesus before the world (Matt 10:33; 22:11f). Paradoxically, Matthew says: To deny "others" is to deny Jesus, is to deny the God who sent Jesus (cf. Matt 10:40-42). This relationship is so intimately bound up in the relationship with "the other" as the "self" that whoever does not take up the suffering human condition and follow Jesus will not be worthy of the Name (Matt 10:38). To identify with the Name of Jesus requires that one "walk" his way; moving continually from the known to the unknown in faith.

When the community of believers gather together in the Name, Jesus assures them of his Presence: "I am in their midst" (Matt 18:20). The transformation process that takes place in the Name may require a radical loss of life or a gradual diminishment of life in this world through the service of "the other" as the "self." There may be hatred, envy and trials of many kinds (Matt 10:22, 27; 24:9). But one loses life in this world only to be blessed with more and more life at the time of the future judgment, when one is found by God (Matt 10:39-42; 27:32). The Gentiles, too, place their hope in this Jesus who bears the Name and the Spirit of God (Matt 12:21 = Isa 42:1-4). Therefore Matthew can rightfully say that Wisdom impels the Christian community to teach and disciplize as well as baptize in the Name and the authority of God, Jesus and the Holy Spirit, as the ONE SOURCE of divine WISDOM (Matt 28:19-20).

Just as the community can be gathered in the Name, so also the Name has the possibility of dividing and scattering the household (Matt 12:30). "Brother will deliver up brother to death, and the father his child, and children will rise against parents and have them put to death; and you will be hated by all for my Name's sake" (Matt 10:21f). During this religious persecution "do not be anxious about what you are to speak because it is the Spirit of your Father who speaks through you" (Matt 10:20). The tensions within the family relationship would result from Jew and Gentile marriages within the household of the faith; between family members who accept Jesus as the Christ and those who do not identify with the Name. A son betrays his father; a daughter her mother and a daughter-in-law's belief may stand in opposition to that of her mother-in-law's religious belief (Matt 10:35). In Matthew's community one's enemies may be those who believe that exceeding righteousness presents options over and above the letter of the Law. They may even be members of one's own household (Matt 10:36).

To call those of one's household Beelzebul (Matt 10:25) the prince of devils, is not unlike the power and the function of the Name that is attributed to Jesus, who is the Master of the Household (Matt 9:34; 12:26f). If they maligned Jesus, they may also treat the children of the household in like manner. The prophetic note of warning reminds the community to be prepared for total misunderstanding of the way of Wisdom. The *House* that is built by God succumbs to the elements and the weathering of time, and needs continual renovation by the divine architect.

TEACHER OF THE HOUSE

During his historical ministry, Jesus identified himself exclusively as THE TEACHER (Matt 26:18). It is only after his departure as Risen Lord that his function is given to the disciples: ". . . teach the nations (Gentiles) to observe all that I have commanded you" (Matt 28:20). Implicit in the commission of Jesus is the statement about his own identity before God and in the presence of the Christian community: "You are not to be called Rabbi for you have ONE TEACHER" (Matt 23:8). And Jesus also instructs the community of followers that there is ONE MASTER of this household (Matt 10:25) who is THE CHRIST (Matt 23:10). It is in and through this progressive understanding of the unity of the community that Jesus illustrates his message by using the divine similitude: no student is above THE TEACHER; no servant is above THE MASTER. It would be more than satisfactory if the students were *like* their teacher and the servants *like* their one master, the Christ (Matt 10:24f).

Jesus was also recognized by the crowds, the Scribes and the Pharisees as a teacher who taught with authority (Matt

7:28f; 9:11; 12:38). Even the Herodians (Matt 17:24) and the Sadducees were perplexed by the new interpretations and his teaching regarding the Law (Matt 22:16, 24, 36). They acknowledged his teaching as true and acknowledged Jesus as the one who taught the way of God truthfully (Matt 22:16). However, official Judaism did not recognize Jesus as THE CHRIST, and continued to question the freedom that Jesus exercised concerning the Law and its precepts (Matt 16:12; 22:23). Jesus advocated keeping the commandments of God in preference to the traditions that were instituted as doctrines by the official teachers within Judaism. It was this teaching that Jesus presented openly in their synagogues (Matt 4:23; 9:35; 13:54), in their cities (Matt 11:1) and in the temple (Matt 21:23; 26:55).

To give some indication of the source of his teaching, Jesus makes it clear that as members of this family on earth, all peoples are brothers and sisters under the ONE Father/Mother in heaven (Matt 23:9). Therefore, the children of the kingdom on earth are rightfully free from the head tax or tribute due to the earthly rulers (Matt 17:24). By identifying Jesus as THE TEACHER within the Christian community of followers, Matthew attempts to teach that the Laws of the land, city, temple can be adapted to the contemporary situation. Yet it was this new teaching and his divine authority that brought Jesus to his passion and death.

In the final analysis THE TEACHER also directed the events of his life as they are played out within the membership of the house of Israel: "I will keep the Passover at *your house* with my disciples" indicating the present as the precise moment for which Jesus had come. "My time is at hand" (Matt 26:18). In his passage to the kingdom of his Father in heaven, Jesus would drink the fruit of the vine *anew*. "That day" is the day of the messianic banquet when heaven and earth, the divine and the human are covenanted anew. It is the *new age* of salvation (Matt 1:21) that day of God's forgiving love (Matt 26:28), the age in which we live.

CHILDREN OF THE HOUSE

One of the greatest blessings bestowed upon the household of believers in this *new age* of salvation is the gift of *new life*. Children constitute this blessing (Matt 19:13f) which witnesses to God's promise fulfilled to Abraham through all generations (Gen 12:1-3; Hos 11:1; Ps 127:3ff). But John the Baptist reminds his people that God is able to raise up progeny to Abraham from stones (Matt 3:9). In this *new age*, according to Matthew, God comes to Israel as the child Jesus to mediate life's saving mysteries (Matt 1:21). The humility of this child graphically teaches the lesson on discipleship: "The most exalted will be brought low (Matt 23:12) and the greatest will be your servants (Matt 23:11); even Jesus who gave his life as a ransom for many" (Matt 20:26-28). Therefore, the family Name lives on through the children who are baptized into this household of God (Matt 28:18-20).

To participate in the family Name it is required first of all that children of the household show obedience to the parents (Matt 18:2-4). "For God commanded, 'Honor your father and your mother' and the one who speaks evil of father or mother, let that one surely die'" (Matt 15:4f). A child has the capability to enjoy the present moment and play at things without any real power over life and death, and with little comprehension of joy or sorrow (Matt 11:16). Even though the child may be self-willed or need discipline, the cultivation of character requires years of training to produce the fruitful deeds that reflect a change of mind and heart (Matt 3:8). But Israel's tradition and Wisdom writings have taught her that in and through the experiences of life, one is taught the Will of God (1 Sam 1:4; Dt 4:9; 11:19; Prov 4:1ff). Although Judaism lays principal stress upon instruction in the Law, especially for the young boys, Jesus does not differentiate between the members of the household. "The one who does the Will of my Father in heaven (Matt 7:21) is my brother and sister and mother" (Matt 12:50). Nor does Jesus differentiate the laws that specify the Will of God; God's Wisdom and commandment is ONE for all peoples and for all time (Matt 22:38-40). The one Love/Will of God/self/others is most vividly portrayed in the garden scene: "Father, if it is possible, take this cup from me; yet not as I will but as you will" (Matt 26:39).

The image of the child as it is featured in Matthew's Gospel may symbolize the lack of maturity as well as the social position of those who are welcomed into the House of Wisdom. Chronologically speaking, the child suggests one who has most recently arrived and received gracious hospitality at the family board: "And they all ate and were satisfied." But Matthew also states primarily and specifically, "Besides women and children there were five and four thousand men" (cf Matt 14:21; 15:38). The Gentiles, too, have come in to dine although they have had little instruction and training. As children, the members of this Christian community are under the guidance of the Master until the world comes of age. Perhaps the traditional observers consider the social status of the Gentile communities as falling short of kingdom expectations. These children have had no moral rearing or cultural training in the Law of Moses. But according to Matthew's Gospel, they too, are under the tutelage and guardianship of the Wisdom Teacher until the end of time when Jesus, as God, ultimately

judges the "way of life" of the members of the household of
believers (Matt 25:31-46). Wisdom also plays its personal
relational role in the judgment scene: "Truly, I say to you, as
you did it to one of the least of these my brethren, you did it to
me" (Matt 25:40).

DISCIPLINE OF THE HOUSE

The standard discipline worthy of the House of Wisdom is
symbolized by the yoke of meekness and love. That is, where
"the self" gives place to "the other," one's own yoke is easy
and the burden is light (cf. Matt 11:29f). The ritual law and
the prescriptions of the authorities have become too heavy for
the people to bear. In this context Jesus invites everyone to
come and lodge in Wisdom's school of life's experiences. In the
midst of labor and daily toil, under the heavy burdens of
suffering, false accusations and slander, there is another "way":
it is the "way of Jesus." "Come to me . . . learn from me, for I
am *meek* and *humble* of heart" (Matt 11:29).

Because the term *meek* is used infrequently in the Old
Testament and found only in Matthew among the Gospel
writers, it deserves attention. Moses, the one outstanding
name and person singled out in the Pentateuch or TORAH to
be entrusted with the Law is praised by God as being the *meek*
one, the servant entrusted with *all of God's house.* It is said that
God spoke to this prophet mouth to mouth (cf. Num 12:3, 7).
The mediator of the Law of God is the MEEK ONE who had a
personal encounter with God.

Within the context of four other prophetic passages, the
message regarding the *meek* pertains to the "day of Yahweh" of
the time of the end. Likewise, two of these prophecies specifically equate the *meek* person with the *humble* person. Con-

cerning "those days" Isaiah reminds Israel that the inhabitants who are puffed up in the lofty city will be humbled and the city will be laid low. The footsteps of the *meek* and the *humble* will trample on the people as well as the city when both are brought down from their exalted heights (cf. Isa 26:5f). However, the prophet Zephaniah proclaims that persons who are *meek* and *humble* will be left in the midst of God's people and those who are left in Israel will not do unrighteous deeds nor utter lies or deceitful things (Zeph 3:12). But Joel offers a solution concerning "that day" of the Lord urging them to bring together those who are at enmity and those who dispute among themselves. The battle will be fought without weapons because God's warriors are the *meek* (cf. Joel 3:11).

The culmination of these prophecies is witnessed in the proclamation of Zechariah fulfilled in Jesus: "Behold your king comes to you; triumphant and victorious is he, *meek* and riding on an ass" (Matt 21:5 = Zech 9:9). This lowly pack animal bears the yoke of Jesus who upon coming into his city, is acclaimed with shouts of praise by the lowly ones residing in the midst of Jerusalem: "Hosanna to the Son of David! Blessed is he who comes in the Name of the Lord" (Matt 21:9; 23:39). Indeed, Wisdom's children cried out with the eyes of faith and with Wisdom's insight.

According to Matthew's view of salvation history, "all the prophets and the law prophesied until John" (Matt 11:13). As figure of the prophet-like-Elijah, John the Baptist links the old and the new age and ushers in the new age of the Wisdom of God. In the old age one's foes were designated the tax collectors and sinners, the people associated with the untutored Gentiles. But in the new age of the House of Wisdom: "Wisdom is justified by her *deeds* (Matt 11:19). In this end-time or the new age, the age of Wisdom (salvation), Jesus relates to outsiders and associates with all peoples as members of his own household.

In Matthew's Gospel, the standard rule or "way" of discipline of the *House* has become the way of the *meek*. Wisdom now has taken on the character and the law of every land and culture because in Jesus, it has taken on the face of the human person. It is in and through Jesus that God speaks to humankind face to face.

Jesus lightens the weight of the external rituals or burdens of the Law and focuses on the liberation of the human heart and the human spirit through relationship and service to "the other." The identity of "the other" as "friend" is one whom the Jewish authorities would exclude from the "way of righteousness" because of nationality and/or religion. Wisdom laments this standard of the "way": "I send you prophets, wise persons and scribes; some of them you shall kill and crucify, some of them you shall scourge in your synagogues and persecute from city to city. Behold your city will be left to you desolate" (Matt 23:34, 38).

Indeed, this prophecy is fulfilled in Jesus, Wisdom's standard yoke-bearer who trains others by his lived-example. The true Son of God and King of Israel does not abandon the yoke. Though taunted and reviled, Jesus did not come down from his cross (Matt 27:40, 42), Jesus has also given this disciplinary word to his students and to all who wish to be followers: "Take up your cross and follow me" (Matt 10:38; 16:34). The *meek* persons give heed to this message of Wisdom.

Wisdom invites:

> "Draw near to me, you who are untaught, and lodge
>   in my school.
> Why do you say you are lacking these things, and
>   why are your souls very thirsty?

I opened my mouth and said, Get these things for
   yourselves without money.
Put your neck under the yoke, and let your souls
   receive instruction; it is to be found close by.
See with your eyes that I have labored little
   and found for myself much rest.
Get instruction with a large sum of silver, and
   you will gain by it much gold.
May your soul rejoice in God's mercy and may you
   not be put to shame when you praise God.
Do your work before the appointed time, and
   in God's time, God will give you your reward."

(Sir 51:23-30)

PRAYER IN THE HOUSE

"It is written: My house shall be called a house of prayer"
(Matt 21:13 = Isa 56:7 = Jer 7:11). Children of the house of
Wisdom pray then like this:

"OUR FATHER WHO ART IN HEAVEN
HALLOWED BE THY NAME
THY KINGDOM COME
THY WILL BE DONE on earth as it is in heaven."

(Matt 6:9-10)

The prayer of the Christian community, the OUR FATHER,
may be called the model of the spirit of prayer. The model set
before us by Jesus has given us ultimately a renewed faith in
God. Wisdom asks for one thing: that OUR WILL may be
God's life on earth as it is in heaven. Maybe this suggestion of
Jesus gives some insight into the place and the need as well as
the accomplishment of prayer. Maybe persons are invited to
pray in the manner of the Jews to remind the people of God
that it is not enough to believe that there is a God in heaven

who is concerned about us and who knows our every need before we ask. The people on earth who have God for a loving Father/Mother and who have a goal and a purpose in life need to be reminded that the Will of God establishes a relationship for life here and hereafter. But what is accomplished by prayer?

Six petitions seem to form themselves into a pattern set down in the words of Jesus. What appears to be six petitions, in reality, is one grand request or acclamation of "WILLS":

> "MAY YOUR NAME be held holy
> MAY YOUR KINGDOM COME
> MAY YOUR WILL BE DONE on earth as it is in heaven
> GIVE US this day our daily bread
> FORGIVE US our debts as we forgive our debtors
> DO NOT BRING US to the test, but DELIVER US from evil.
> (Matt 6:9-13)

Just as the ONE GREAT COMMANDMENT of LOVE is featured under the two aspects of love of God and love of neighbor as the self, so also the first three petitions center on OUR WILL desiring to be united with the ONE WILL of God under the aspects of God's NAME, KINGDOM AND WILL. The second set of three requests focuses on OUR WILL under the aspects of God's gift of the necessities for our life in this world as one with the WILL OF GOD. In these six petitions we recognize the ONE WILL intimately bound up in the ONE WILL and the ONE LOVE of God/self/others.

How does this prayer differ from the Jewish Prayer, "the Shema": "Hear O Israel! The Lord Our God is One"? In the Old Testament, God was thought of under the patriarchal image of FATHER of the people of Israel. And Israel, the faithful people of God, were reckoned as the children of God. The prayer that Jesus models and presents to us in Matthew's

Gospel fosters the new familial way of approaching God, a universal summons, that invokes God in prayer as "OUR FATHER."

We are reminded that just as God is ONE, so also humankind is ONE in Jesus, true Israelite and true Son of God (Matt 2:15; 3:17; 4:3, 6; 8:29; 14:33; 16:16; 17:5; 26:63; 27:40, 43, 54). In God's Wisdom, Jesus, Wisdom Incarnate is the One who embodies the Presence of God-with-us. We can, then, indeed pray in and through Jesus to "OUR FATHER" because all peoples of all nations, Jews and Gentiles alike, are privileged to pray this one prayer as one family under God. All are brothers and sisters in Jesus. The family of the pray-ers who have accepted Jesus, is recognized as the community symbolized by the poor, the sick, the blind and the lame. Those who freely accept the good news that Jesus has taught us, know that in this way the kingdom of heaven is brought near. It is the further responsibility of the evangelist Matthew to communicate that God, the Lord of heaven, has come to be with us as Jesus, Son of God on earth (Matt 1:21-23).

Matthew uses the title "Father" with the designation of place, "who art in heaven" to distinguish God from the ancestral Fathers on earth: our Fathers Abraham, Isaac and Jacob. "Father," a primal word in the history of the cultures and religions of the Ancient Near East, is more than just a begetter. Father denotes the creative source, the initiator, the protector, the nourisher of "life." However, the biblical people have no problem representing the feminine aspects of God analogous to Mother and nurse (Isa 44:2, 24; 49:15; 66:12-13) as well as God, imaged as feminine Wisdom, who is lover and wife (Eccl 11:5; Sir 15:2).

The ambiguous concept of God interpreted by the word "Father" in an age of questioning and doubt about the experience or lack of the experience of a human father, may present a problem in our society today. Likewise, the image of the maleness of God at the core of one's faith-life has proved alienating for many women who experience themselves as separated and excluded from worship by a predominance of male role-models. Even changing the Old Testament Father-image to the Son in the Christian tradition has established a barrier for women who find it difficult to identify with the male-image of Jesus Christ as mediator.

While we remain sensitive to women's efforts to liberate God and themselves, our language and relationships continue to create division and misunderstanding. There seems to be no ready solution to this dilemma at the present time other than to recognize in it an age of transition, not unlike that of the first century. Yet Jesus provides the option of WISDOM. One wonders if the experience of Matthew's community was vastly different from the reality of the human condition today!

God, the true author and originator of life in this world resides in heaven. Thus, the proper Name for God is "the Holy One." It is our expressed will that God's Name be held Holy" (Matt 6:9). Our sense of reverence and awe for the Name and the fact that we can acknowledge it already indicates that we give God the proper place and NAME in relationship to our lives. God is "HOLY" and there is no other Holy One. God is totally "other" than ourselves and bears this honorific Divine Name/Place.

God may be said to *make* his/her Name Holy by means of God's manifest saving power and action on behalf of Israel in history. In the old dispensation the people of God sometimes profaned the Name of God. In the new dispensation, God manifested this Holiness and *makes* the Name Holy in Jesus. Jesus reveals the history of God's saving Presence in this world. However, in Matthew's Gospel, Jesus manifests principally and primarily God's Wisdom Incarnate, and in God's Wisdom, the kingdom of heaven has come to earth. God's Will for "Life" has become manifest in SOPHIA (WISDOM). In God's Wisdom, life in this world has taken on new meaning in and through the life, death and resurrection of Jesus. It is in living out our will that our life will make known God's Presence through the Name of the Holy Ones of God.

Therefore, we pray, expressing OUR WILL: "May your kingdom come," synonymous with "may your will be done on earth as it is in heaven" (Matt 6:10)! God's Name, Kingdom and Will are three paradoxical aspects of the ONE TRUTH: God, the transcendent "HOLY ONE" is with us and God wills to remain with us until the end of time. In the acknowledgement of God's Presence with us and in the acceptance of our humanness, we pray that God's Will may come to "life" on earth as in heaven. This one supreme movement of heaven to earth comes about in every adult choice we make and every mature decision that is ours. To freely make our will the manifestation of God's life in this world as Jesus did and continues to do in us, is the prerogative of WISDOM. Jesus extended God's manifest love and freedom to all peoples through the offer of discipleship. Jesus is the primary instrument of God's Will and God's Love. Our humanness extends this interior, eternal and universal manifestation of God's life to all. The will of the adult chooses God-Father/Mother over any other strange gods that we make for ourselves and the lesser gods that we make of ourselves.

To unite our will with the Will of God is not a question of resigning ourselves to the Will of God but of choosing our "life-time" as the extension of God's "HOUR" on earth. When we take our lives into our hands, acknowledging our life as

"gift," each day as "our hour" is a time of decision and choice.
God is at the center of all our relationships and thoughts,
making the "ONE WILL" of God *our will.*

The last three petitions, as they are called, present our daily
needs and our daily requirements. But is there a need for this
kind of prayer? Matthew suggests that Jesus confronts the
community with the startling announcement that God knows
what is needed before one even asks. And he even goes so far as
to say: "For the Gentiles seek all these things; and your
heavenly Father knows that you need them all" (Matt 6:32).
But "Seek first God's kingdom and God's righteousness, and
all these things shall be yours as well" (Matt 6:33). Then why
pray?

Jesus prays to God in the most familiar way as "My Father"
(Matt 26:39, 42, 44). And in the most dire situation of
suffering and death, Jesus prays that God's Will be done (Matt
26:36, 44). A cry for help and salvation in a situation of
deprivation and loss is essentially a fear of the loss of "self."
Jesus was a human being who did not come to perform before
us but to reveal to us what it means to unite the human and
the divine Will. This is modeled in Jesus' Word and Deed. It
also expresses what it means to pray. The sense of loss and
relinquishment of this earthly realm is as much a death-
resistance experience in Jesus' Sophia existence as it is for us.
But once the relationship of the human with the divine Will
wedded in prayer begins to grasp the freedom of this union of
WILLS, one discovers what life is all about. Then the "ego-self"
that struggles to control this world gives free reign to the
"true-self" directed by God's Wisdom and Love. This surrender to God of the same flesh and blood, the same life
principle, that has given meaning and purpose to Jesus' life,
becomes the real purpose of our existence: God/self/others. If

there is one temptation in life, it is to withhold from God what belongs to God. True prayer allows us to reclaim God in this life on earth through FAITH. We are not permitted to deprive God of what is God's due and make the HOUSE OF PRAYER a den of robbers (Matt 21:13).

Members of the House of Wisdom pray in faith, never doubting that with God the impossible can become possible (Matt 17:21; 21:21f). Prayer for persecutors bears the transformative power to change the "self," as well as the situation of the "other." Even the self-destructive forces of hatred and revenge can be transformed through prayer, making love possible; specifically, love of the enemy. Faith and love act as the fuel of the House of Prayer enabling us to acknowledge that we are all children of the ONE GOD. As children of "OUR FATHER in heaven," we perceive that the same benefactions of love are poured out on the just and the unjust, making prayer in faith all the more compulsory. The Lord's Prayer unites all in their true allegiance to God as members of the one household (Matt 5:44). This is the purpose of prayer: to unite us with God/self/others in one mind and heart.

The Prayer "OUR FATHER" associates us with all persons whom Wisdom perceives as related to us by the mere fact of our humanness. We may never see them or know them personally, but we are confident that prayer will disclose "self" to ourselves so that we can become more and more the believers in a God whom we do not see but who we believe unites us to the "other." The human and the earthly in us fears for our life and our work, forgetting that our life's energies are directed toward losing our life (the perception of our "self" as separated from God) so that God's Will/Love/Life may be found in us. The unwillingness to accept God's fatherhood/ motherhood will deny us the unlimited love which is God's

Will for us. Our love and forgiveness can aspire to be as boundless as God's because it is God's love and God's life in us that we project and extend into this world.

Even though the community prays at stated times and keeps holy the Sabbath or the Lord's Day, Wisdom Incarnate exemplifies the importance of personal prayer. Jesus slips away from the crowd and from his disciples to pray (Matt 14:23; 26:36). He encourages prayer in secret, in one's private chamber, where one is liberated from the communal pressures that may force one to pay only lip service to God (Matt 15:18f). He advocates individual prayer, offering the silence to discern the voice within one's own heart, freeing the person to communicate with God, which is prayer's unique experience and its own reward (Matt 6:3-7).

What does prayer accomplish if we are told not to worry about what we are to eat and drink? We are not to be anxious about the daily needs because God knows that we have need even before we ask (Matt 6:25-33). Life is more than these externals and today's needs are sufficient (Matt 6:34) when one seeks the kingdom and God's due righteousness. It would seem that the purpose of the prayer is not to get or even to ask for "things." It is rather to acknowledge the gifts and the absolute necessities of life that we have received: the wisdom to know the ONE WILL and the ONE LOVE of God manifest in Jesus who lived this human condition. Wisdom makes this equality of relationship and sharing of our resources in the service of others possible—rather essential—for our daily life.

Those who believe in the Presence of "God-with-us" can pray as a community of the people of God to the ONE GOD as OUR FATHER in heaven. Jews and Gentiles alike secure heaven for themselves as the one place of the illusive presence where "THE NAME" is set apart for this relationship. But the kingdom of heaven is not confined to temporal or eternal boundaries. Prayer is a way of asserting God's nearness. As an apt form of communicating with God, prayer arouses the depths of our being. The way to approach God in prayer is to look within our heart and mind and say the words of the prayer: OUR FATHER—OUR KINGDOM COME—OUR WILL BE DONE on earth as it is in heaven.

As a community of believers we dare to say this prayer with confidence and trust that when we ask, seek and knock, it will be opened to us because it is God's Will that no one be lost, that all be saved. It is God's Will that Jews and Gentiles enter the kingdom that unites all as ONE in the ONE WILL of God. Therefore we pray that OUR WILL will be done on earth.

The "OUR FATHER" as the prayer of Jesus models the maturity that is required to distance from the child in us and to be able to see God and claim ourselves in the union and the choice or decisions of WILLS. Our will is separated and apart from the God who is utterly transcendent and yet intimately bound up with the "wisdom" that is within us to transform the earthly into the heavenly through the word of WISDOM— as GOD'S WILL. Forgiving our debtors as we are forgiven is one salvific action before God. By forgiving the other, we acknowledge the forgiveness that we have received. Debt is more than sin, it is the obligation that we owe to God for the forgiving love that has brought us together again as one family and as children of the one source and origin of all life. What is due to God is the corresponding gift and the obligation that we have to forgive as we have been forgiven (Matt 18:23f; 6:12, 14f). What we acknowledge as gift received can then be freely given (Matt 10:8).

On the last day, the day of judgment, we will be asked to give an account of the debt we owe to the other because of the cancellation of the debt we owed to God. If God has cancelled all our debts should we not also forgive and cancel the differences that we have with one another? The human is the counterpart of the divine in the one great commandment and the one great union of WILLS. The love that we have received is the LOVE THAT IS FREELY GIVEN. Jesus therefore asks in the parable of the wicked servant: "I forgave you all the debt because you besought me; should you not have had mercy on your fellow servant, as I had mercy on you?...So also my heavenly Father will do to everyone of you, if you do not forgive your brother/sister from your heart" (Matt 18:32-35). So essential and so utterly basic is this truth for the Christian community of Matthew's day, that he adds a rider to the prayer that confirms its importance for the Jews and the Gentiles: "For if you forgive others their trespasses, your heavenly Father also will forgive you; but if you do not forgive others their trespasses, neither will your Father forgive your trespasses" (Matt 6:14-15). Our will is assuredly God's life and God's action in this world. God depends upon us to witness to this unity of relationship through forgiveness.

If our prayer petitions a union of wills, and if we pray that OUR WILL may be God's LIFE in this world, we no longer need worry or be anxious about pleasing others, feeling guilty or less loving when it comes to a true response of what Matthew speaks of as exceeding righteousness. No longer need we fear a God "out there," a God who threatens or is to be avoided; a God who imposes demands and requirements upon us from above or outside ourselves that we may be unable to fulfill. The person imbued with the Spirit of exceeding righteousness looks for ways and means to please the God who is within, and discovers in the seeking and the finding that God is heard and believed within the self. The person whose actions are done in faith, not knowing but following the way of revelation and insight—is a child of WISDOM. And God's child is Wisdom Incarnate—the human in us who enables us to call and address God as "OUR FATHER/MOTHER."

It is the essential privilege of our humanity that we are the source of our own actions! We are not just programmed and planned or moved from place to place. God has given us the freedom to choose and decide for or against God/self/others. God is utterly free and allows us to be so utterly free as to shape our lives to the point where we are free to choose "our will," forgive others and feel comfortable in choosing our will over and above any other will but God's. This is the kind of God we have, and the God whom we are privileged to call "OUR FATHER!"

There is no outside power or force that can coerce us into acting against our will. We are free. Only the God within us has the ability to act upon us from within. No external force or power can exert any dominion over us unless we freely choose to let this god persuade us from the outside. The effectiveness of the prayer of Jesus lies in this: we are free to CHOOSE OUR WILL—knowing that we have freely chosen GOD. God's Will is the Master/Lord of our life and we cannot and will not serve two masters (Matt 6:24).

Christianity has never been too comfortable with asserting "my will" or too confident with doing "my will" as an axiomatic statement of the mature Christian and adult choices. It has been equally as mystifying to know God's Will and to be assured that what we are doing is the Will of God. To bring these "WILLS" into agreement, to feel confident that the happiness and the freedom, the fullness of life and hope that we experience is the WILL OF GOD, it is necessary to pray. To offer to unite my will with the other and with God and to believe that "OUR WILL" is confidently merged with the Will of God is the prayer of the believer. This prayer plants within human persons the appreciation of what it means to be children of WISDOM. The mature Christian requires a deeper faith, a merciful heart, and a profound realization that as we judge so shall we be judged and that the measure we measure will be meted out to us in the end-time judgment (Matt 7:1f).

When Jesus reminds the community that it should pray — not as the Gentiles with many words in order to be heard — not as the hypocrites who pay lipservice but with distracted heart, far from the God to whom they pray, he is asking for a superabundant FAITH, MERCY, and JUDGMENT (Matt 23:23) that summarizes what WISDOM AND PRAYER is all about in Matthew's vision of the *House of Wisdom*.

6

Presence:
The Fulfillment of
Prophetic Expectations of the Kingdom
(Matt 8-10)

Forgiveness

The prophets served to remind the covenant community about its obligation to live justly in accordance with the Law. When this obligation and command is fulfilled, the will of God, as expressed through the word of the prophets, is realized in the lives of the people Israel:

> "Say to those who are of fearful heart,
>   'Be strong fear not!
> Behold, your God will come with vengeance
>   With the recompense of God
> God will come and save you.'
>
> Then the eyes of the blind shall be opened,
>   And the ears of the deaf unstopped;
> then shall the lame man leap like a hart,
>   and the tongue of the dumb sing for joy."

(Isa 35:4-6a)

For Matthew's community, miraculous cures, healings, and exorcisms are signs of the fulfillment of Israel's prophetic expectations of the kingdom. Conversely, sickness, paralysis, blindness and demonic possession serve as prophetic warnings.

Evidently, something had gone wrong with God's creation; Israel had not kept faith with the covenant. Disordered harmony in nature and a lack of physical well-being, or illness, were the consequences of Israel's perverse ways. Failure to observe the Law was disobedience toward God, and the just and good God must, in justice, punish the sinner or evil-doer. This is how the prophetic voice reminds Israel of the very close connection between sin and disease. The evil in this world manifests God's punishment for sin. This had been the prophetic reminder and Israel's understanding of God in covenant relationship. The wisdom of the sages also affirmed that the person who suffered was exposed as a sinner even if the sin was done in secret.

Jesus revealed the divine perspective. God is not punishing Israel by afflicting her with disease, suffering and death. God is neither alienated nor distanced from creation, which is born of steadfast love. God is with us as a forgiving God. And thus, forgiveness is the fulfillment of the prophetic expectation of the kingdom.

Matthew begins chapters 8 and 9 with an allusion to the prophets' announcement of the end-time pilgrimage of the peoples to Zion: "Jesus came down from the mountain and crowds followed him" (Matt 8:1). The narrative is set for God's salvific act in the coming of the reign of Jesus in Jerusalem. Matthew is prepared to tell the community what faith discloses to them: God's power is in Jesus to change Israel's understanding of suffering as punishment for sin and sin as separation from God.

In chapter 10 Matthew carries the Jewish Christian community a step further, by challenging the community to identify totally with Jesus, the Teacher and the Master. He calls them to discipleship, to a right relationship with God in Jesus, to a change of mind and to be messengers of peace/forgiveness.

Jesus teaches in the Jewish synagogues, preaches the good news of the kingdom and heals every disease and every infirmity among the people (Matt 4:23; 9:35). "They brought him all the sick, those afflicted with various diseases and pain, demoniacs, epileptics, and paralytics and he healed them" (Matt 4:24). These words of prophetic fulfillment are Matthew's sublime testimony to the community's faith and prayer, and to God's forgiveness and liberation. They summarize the mission of Jesus (Savior) who saves the people from their sins (cf. Matt 1:21; 26:27).

What is sin and how is it identified? Matthew does not define sin nor does he describe it. Through the personal encounters that Jesus has along the way, the true nature of sin is revealed. Encounters with Jesus in faith provide the new age answer to the question: Who are the saved? The ones who are forgiven.

Persons with many differing beliefs and various traditional backgrounds are freed by Jesus to participate in the community of believers. This is the salvation that the Jews were expecting. It is in the encounter with the person of Jesus that healing takes place or that sin is forgiven. The faith of individuals meets the forgiveness and liberation of Jesus.

FORGIVENESS AND FAITH

How does Matthew convey this message of salvation and forgiveness? Matthew structures the miracle events around three categories of people. The first group of persons encountering Jesus can be categorized as those outside the official cultic practices of Judaism and who, by virtue of their suffering human condition, look to the future for possibilities of new life. Three individuals who have no official or legal status within the ranks of Judaism approach Jesus: the leper who is an outcast because of his physical and moral condition of sin; the centurion who is a non-Jew and bears no religious right to the power of the Jewish Jesus to heal; and the woman who has no voice in this society and makes no claims upon Jesus (Matt 8:1-17). These people have no association or relationship to the official Jewish religious structures. Judaism offers them no status and affords them no identity as functional members within the religious or social sphere.

The second set of persons who encounter Jesus are those who believe in the presence of the Risen Lord, but fear puts limits on their ability to enter into a faith relationship with Jesus: the disciples who share the earthly lot with Jesus, set sail with him in the boat, and are threatened by the sea; the Gadarene demoniacs who recognize the power and authority of Jesus, and the people who encounter Jesus and beg him to leave the territory; the paralytic who is borne before Jesus because of the faith of his friends (Matt 8:13-9:8). Jesus startles them all by his saving word of forgiveness and healing. These faith-filled people are aware of their relationship to Jesus but in a moment of anxiety and apprehension, fear overtakes them in his presence. Fear seems to dominate faith.

A third group consists of those who are rooted in the

traditional beliefs of Judaism; past history is their basis for judgments on the present. They are pleasantly surprised that their traditional past is caught up in the salvific act of faith now that the new age is present. In Jesus, all people stand in the time of the END. To all who have faith in him, the new age is present and new life is offered as forgiveness.

The daughter of the official synagogue ruler had died. Jesus was asked to come to his house so that she would live. On the way, a woman with a flow of blood, presuming upon the healing power of Jesus, transgresses the Law by touching the hem of his garment. (She was considered unclean and defiled according to the code of Leviticus). As Jesus continues his journey, incongruously, it is two blind men and one dumb man who identify Jesus as son of David and receive the prophetic word of healing (Matt 9:18-33).

In summary, the persons who have faith, the believers who are fearful, and the faithful followers of Judaism are all seeking the one vision of life that leads to the goal. The goal is the kingdom, and the goal of all life is God. Faith in the kingdom present, the search for God which Matthew depicts as forgiveness is an encounter with Jesus, "God-with-us." The recipients of the healing miracles were praised for their confident faith. Faith is of the essence of human life and is expressed in many forms. All those who encounter Jesus have faith which can be equated with prayer. It is the prayer of faith that brings forgiveness/healing; an immediate response and action on the part of Jesus. Prayer in faith opens the believer to God's love.

FORGIVENESS IN PRAYER

In the dialogue between the person and Jesus, the request for forgiveness becomes a prayer (word) in faith that the power of God in Jesus will cure. Therefore, Jesus is addressed as LORD. Nothing distracts the believer from this intimate communion of mind and heart; "Lord, if you will . . ." and "Lord, I am not worthy . . . only say the word." The true prayer of dialogue with God is a union of wills, as Jesus taught us in the Lord's prayer: "Thy will be done on earth as it is in heaven" (Matt 6:9-13), and in Gethsemane: "But not as I will but as you will" (Matt 26:37).

In the healing ministry of Jesus, encounters point to a relationship of Jesus with the person who is not apologetic about his/her condition, or position, as an outsider in the community of Israel. The person makes known the need for healing—to be made whole—which implies forgiveness that is personal and may have social implications: ". . .forgive us . . . as we forgive . . ." (Matt 6:12). Physical and spiritual well-being affect the total human condition. What concerns one person may have ramifications for many other persons. What alienates anyone from God/self/others is the nature of sin. Therefore, the encounters that life offers are not to be taken lightly. In order to know God's will for us, forgiveness is to be lived in faith/prayer or dialogue with Jesus. Faith conquers the sin-boundaries that have defined us: religious boundaries (leper); national boundaries (centurion); social boundaries (woman). In these miracle accounts, Matthew discloses what the sin is that divides God from humankind. Is there, perhaps, security in division and separation? The presence and word of Jesus create wholeness, not separation nor alienation. Fear is the only inhibiting factor.

FORGIVENESS AND FEAR

Fear permeates the environment in which the three subsequent miracles take place. Fear rises from the demonic forces or the waters of chaos that surround and control our circumstances and our society. The herdsmen of the swine were in utmost fear when they recognized Jesus. They asked him to leave their neighborhood. The paralytic is carried by his friends into the presence of Jesus. Seeing their faith, Jesus forgives the man his sin. Therefore, he has the authority to say "your sins are forgiven," "rise and walk," or "take up your bed and go into your house." These are three ways of expressing the same truth. Suffering/sickness is healed; sin and the power of the evil spirit are now broken and the prophetic time of salvation is at hand. Strangely enough, the crowds, seeing Jesus conquer the power of sin, are afraid (Matt 9:8). But the authority of Jesus on earth (as in heaven) is to forgive sin. Faith conquers the forces of fear. All who encounter Jesus in faith are forgiven and enter into the kingdom/presence of God.

Although the institution of Judaism had made rather restrictive legislation concerning who could come into the presence of God (into the temple, into the synagogue, and into the land), Jesus, the God-presence, reveals the manner in which the God-act frees and liberates all those who desire to be saved.

FORGIVENESS OF JEWISH BELIEVERS

The three remaining cures are symbolic of salvation within the old institutions of Judaism. The incidents occur in the *house* of Israel. Matthew welcomes Jesus into his *house*. Jesus eats with tax collectors and sinners. He goes to Jairus' *house* and raises the daughter from death to life. The two blind men follow Jesus. They identify Jesus as son of David and when Jesus enters the *house,* he asks the blind men for an expression of their faith. "Do you believe that I am able to do this? And the fame of Jesus was spread throughout the *land"* (Matt 9:28, 31).

The *house* of David and the *land* of Israel are symbolic of the authority and the power Jesus exercises over the community of Jewish believers. In the presence of Jesus the end-time blessings promised by the prophets have come to pass. The two blind men (witnesses) of Israel see, and the dumb man speaks. Never was there anything like this *seen* in Israel. But the community members are free to accept or reject, and the Pharisees say: "He casts out demons by the Prince of demons" (Matt 9:34). Jewish Christianity and Judaism (the two houses), and the kingdom of God and the kingdom of the world (the two powers) are in conflict.

Throughout the narratives of chapters 8 and 9 the prophetic aspects of healing are obvious. The visible reality of a cure is clear to the scribes and the Pharisees. The invisible healing, forgiveness of sin, is no less real. The word of God is effective and creative. It makes the person whole; it makes the person new. Forgiveness establishes a new relationship with God in Jesus. The promise of blessing and reward is a possibility for the future. The official representatives of Judaism were afforded the opportunity to recognize the power of Jesus and his respect for the Law. Does healing, the forgiveness of sins, break the Law and at the same time fulfill the prophetic testimony? Even the question regarding fasting is a reminder that the old observance is not taken away, but the practice is informed with new meaning since the coming of the Messiah, the CHRIST (cf. Matt 9:14-17).

Mission

Having clarified for the Jewish Christian community that Jesus is the fulfillment of prophetic expectations of the kingdom, Matthew proceeds to give a view of discipleship which is prophetic. He uses the form of discourse to instruct the community on the mission of the disciples.

DISCIPLESHIP

In Matthew's treatment of discipleship, symbols of prophetic imagery (call, name, sent) abound (Matt 10:1, 2, 5). The disciples are called, names are given, and they are sent to Israel, to the lost sheep, those without a shepherd who have already drawn the compassionate response of Jesus (Matt 9:36; Zech 10:2). The disciples preach the good news of the kingdom as they "go on the way" (Isa 40:3). The prophetic signs of miraculous cures and demonic exorcisms which they perform witness to the messianic mission. Identifying totally with the Teacher and Master is the task, duty and response of the disciple.

In Matthew discipleship is specifically reserved for those who are called by Jesus, who are given instructions and commissioned by him. Those caught up in discipleship are given everything they need to perform the mission of Jesus. They are carefully instructed to take nothing with them along the way: no gold nor silver, not even a few coppers for the journey. They are not to take a spare tunic nor a staff nor footwear. They need nothing to fulfill their office of healing and forgiveness. However, the gift of forgiveness which they have received, they are commissioned to give freely to all whom they encounter along the way and in its many faceted forms (Matt 10:8). The gift given in forgiveness is PEACE. If the gift of peace is accepted, it will be peaceful in the house (church, community, family, society). If it is not, PEACE will return to them (Matt 10:13). Peace in the presence of Jesus points to the recognition that the kingdom of heaven is at hand. How aptly Jesus describes the disciples' ministry of healing/forgiveness as PEACE (Matt 10:16).

This mission of PEACE and the message of forgiveness (by God) will be questioned and attacked in the Jewish Christian communities. For this reason Jesus himself was delivered before the Sanhedrin and flogged. It is possible that this mission of peace will not be accepted by the Jews at Jamnia and so Christians too will be persecuted "for my sake" and hated "for my name's sake" (Matt 10:22)

Persecution and hatred for his name's sake are, therefore, the likely lot of those who bear the name of Jesus as Christians (cf. Matt 10:22). "If they persecuted the prophets and me, they will persecute you because of me" (cf. Matt 5:12). Matthew forewarns them that as disciples in this Jewish Christian community they will be delivered before councils, governors and kings. They will be dragged into the synagogues and before the Gentiles. This betrayal within the household will accomplish a prophetic wonder: "It is not you who speak but the Spirit of your Father speaking in you!" (Matt 10:20). The Father in heaven is bound to you in an intimate relationship. And so the delivering up and the *handing over* to kings and governors and before the Gentiles will only act as a testimony, a witness to Jesus (Matt 10:18). Between Jesus and the disciple, there is a relationship which is best symbolized by the cross. The acceptance of the cross is the sign of following the Teacher/Master. It is the cross that underlines the paradox that the disciple finds life by losing it. The cross is the only suitable sign of the disciple's intimate relationship of life with Jesus, "God-with-us." Disciples can expect their life's witness to be subject to the same afflictions and sufferings as their Master/Teacher and as the prophets of old. As the Teacher, so the disciples! As the Master, so the servants of the household (Matt 10:24f).

For true and faithful disciples and for this Jewish Christian community the prophecy of Mal 4:6 will be experienced with deep sorrow and pain: "I have come to divide households" (Matt 10:35; Mic 7:6). These divisions will reach brother and brother; they will set father against children and children will deliver parents to death. The foes will be within one's own household; all of this in a society in which kinship ties are the most sacred.

Preserving fidelity in the midst of persecution and suffering will yield the disciple a rich reward. The absolute authoritative word of God is spoken through Jesus: "Amen, I say to you: You shall not lose your reward" (Matt 10:42). The enemy to fidelity will be fear but, "Do not be anxious: Do not fear! Do not fear those who persecute or kill the body, fear only him whom you confess or deny . . ." (Matt 10:26-31). One must be worthy of the Master of the house.

The disciples are mandated to preach as they go "on the way" that "the kingdom of heaven is at hand" and to do precisely what Jesus did in healing and casting out demons, etc. (Matt 4:23; 9:35; 10:8f). The healing ministry given to the disciples in prophetic imagery is Matthew's way of saying that sin is forgiven. Sin is the condition in which we normally spend our lives; we live in a so-called separated state, in isolation, in alienation and even division, cut off from God/self/neighbor/world. The message of Jesus in Matthew's Gospel points to the new way of being with God. God is present even in the midst of the strained relationships between Jews and Gentiles. Matthew confirms that there is a new way of seeing life in relationship to God. The kingdom of heaven is the presence of God at hand. The world with all its conflictive situations is the arena, the realm, the place where God has desired to be with us.

Faith in the God who raised Jesus from the dead has allowed us the freedom of mind and heart to look at our world and God's presence differently. We are able to see this earth as the place where the human and the divine are united in one body through the Holy Spirit which is given us. As the Holy Spirit speaks and acts in us, the word of God enables us to recognize the cross and suffering in our society as opportunities to be with God in the mysteries of life. They are no longer darkness and gloom. They are the nights that allow the vision of light and "God-with-us" to shine more brightly.

The mission of the disciples, then, is to reflect in life the testimony and the word of Jesus. The gift of forgiveness and the word of God in Jesus reflect the word of the Father's forgiving love. "It is the sick who need the physician; I have come to call not the JUST but sinners" (Matt 9:13). The message of the disciples is no longer a call to repentance, as it was formerly in John the Baptist's ministry to the Jewish people. Neither is it the same as the call issued by Jesus at the beginning of his public ministry: "Repent! the kingdom of heaven is at hand" (Matt 3:2; 4:17). In his ministry Jesus has fulfilled the mission. In this new age, the disciple is the one who is identified totally with the Teacher and the Master. The Israel of old was given the opportunity to change her mind and heart about the way that she looked upon the presence of the kingdom of God. Disciples are called to the self-same ministry that the prophets foretold: "I desire mercy and not sacrifice"

(Matt 9:13; 12:7; Hos 6:6). Disciples no longer ask others to change their minds, nor do they attack their ways of thinking. Our human standards of judgment no longer apply. Mission is proclamation of the forgiveness of sin in prophetic metaphorical language: "The blind see, the lame walk, lepers are cleansed and the poor have the gospel preached to them" and "Blessed those who are not 'scandalized' by ME!" (Matt 11:5f; 10:8).

The message of Christianity is just as much a 'scandal' in today's world as it was in Matthew's day. There are so many facts distorted, so many deceptions in our own lives, so many destructive forces in our minds and hearts and hands, so much violence and so many divisions in the community of faith — that all the forces of the cosmic powers seem pitted against us. But we are bearers of the mission of Jesus who forgives and makes whole. As believers we need not see the effects of our ministry nor the impact of the forgiveness we offer in the heart of another person. In faith we go along the way, and like Jesus, continue to proclaim the kingdom of heaven at hand. The kingdom, a prophetic image, is the sign of "God-with-us."

The focus of our call to discipleship and ministry of service in the kingdom is forgiveness. The forgiveness that we receive from God through our encounter with Jesus in faith is the gift that we offer. We receive peace in order to give this PEACE to other towns and places where in the END, the Son of Man comes. Even though the mission may not be accomplished according to our intents and purposes, God's forgiveness will be realized. The mission of discipleship is to effect change by living the reality of the kingdom: "God-with-us!" Wherever there are believers, there will be other disciples to minister and to *hand on* the mission of Jesus, the ministry of forgiveness . . . not necessarily in words, but by their lives.

7

Presence:
The Fulfillment of
Wisdom Expectations of the Kingdom
(Matt 11-13)

Discernment

The symbol, kingdom of heaven, derives from the thought world of Jewish apocalyptic and the Aramaic targums that were read in the synagogues of Palestine in Jesus' day. The kingdom is never precisely defined in the Gospels but this term often refers to a future reign of God on earth. It occurs in time, in history and it embraces the political, social and personal dimensions of life. Thus, the kingdom is intended to include all human beings and the entire cosmos.

For Matthew's hearers the kingdom is at hand. Jesus, the Messiah, has inaugurated the presence of the kingdom. This truth of Christian faith has caused division among the household of believers because the presence of Jesus fosters different interpretations of kingdom values and diverse perceptions of God's presence with us.

To address this situation, Matthew superimposes the later experience of divided community upon the kingdom presence in the life of Jesus. If the person of Jesus and his message caused division among his own followers, it is not unlikely that the Christian presence, too, will arouse conflict. This is not a new experience. But division inhibits the process of hearing the message and seeing the kingdom come. Matthew believes that Jesus has offered us another opportunity to hear and consequently to see this kingdom reality in a new way. We could say that the kingdom is itself *one;* it is not divided. The kingdom comprises a diversity of peoples and gifts, with differing viewpoints on how this kingdom reality is apprehended. This new age, an age of wisdom, comes into existence when faith discerns that the kingdom permeates all of reality. The good and the bad, the evil and the just person, will live together in this kingdom until the end of the age. But then, God will enter into judgment with them (Matt 13:40, 49).

Matthew has Jesus begin by questioning the believers regarding their understanding of the Prophets and the Law. Have you heard the traditional teaching and seen Jesus' new interpretation which conveys Wisdom's (God's) perception of the kingdom reality? The parables of chapters 11 and 12 ask this question based on the Prophets and the Law, the factors that have caused division in the household of believers. Chapter 13 answers the question with another question: Have you understood the message of the parables of the kingdom? If you have, then you would have heard that ". . . every scribe who has been trained for the kingdom of heaven is like a householder who brings out of his treasure what is new and what is old" (Matt 13:52). Jewish Christians and their Gentile counterparts are participants in the kingdom as well as the Pharisaic Jews. This is God's wisdom.

The message is old but ever new. Jesus uses questions to draw out the community's understanding of the prophetic images and the Torah teaching. Questions and images offer the hearer the opportunity to integrate the message into his or her own thought and life. With the wisdom of God, Jesus leaves the individual free to respond: "The one who has ears to hear, let that one hear" (Matt 11:15; 13:9, 43). The new and the old teaching is in continuity with the tradition of the *promise* as set forth in the genealogy of Matthew's Gospel, but the word of God in the words of Jesus is forever new. Differing cultures and historical situations offer new insights into the revelation given to us by the words of Jesus. To respond in faith as believers requires a discernment process.

TO SEE AND TO HEAR

In biblical usage, words of seeing and hearing suggest a process of discernment. Discernment is a power to see beyond the evident, beyond external appearances that may deceive or be deceptive to the human eye. The person who discerns has an ability to penetrate beyond the superficial, to penetrate into the mind and heart. The discerner has the ability to read and to see through character or motives, to understand the difference between the action and the motives for the action. Through a process of questioning, discernment provides a person with the insight to know and recognize the distinct and unique place that we call kingdom.

TO HEAR AND TO SEE

In his particular parabolic kingdom instruction, Matthew reverses the formulaic expression *to see and to hear*. Because he challenges the Jewish Christians at a later period in history, he uses the phrase, *to hear and to see*. The community experienced revelation, not by seeing Jesus with bodily eyes as did the first followers of Jesus, but by hearing the word of the gospel (cf Matt 13:16f). This good news of salvation concerning Jesus has come to them by hearing and subsequently seeing with the discernment of faith.

DISCERNMENT REGARDING THE MESSIAH

Because we live by faith and not by sight, the question and answer form offers us a method that enables us to enter into life's discerning process.

The prophet John the Baptist questions Jesus: "Are you he who is to come or shall we look for another?" (Matt 11:13). This question establishes the basis for the Messiah's presence and our quest for life. If Jesus is Israel's expected one, then the new messianic age has arrived. Jesus responds with the prophetic image of fulfillment: "The blind see, the lame walk . . ." Healing implies the forgiveness of sins; salvation from sin was the specific purpose for which Jesus had come (cf. Matt 1:21; 4:23; 9:35; 11:4f).

Faith discerns: am I able to hear and see this mighty work of God as a sign of the Christ's presence? The variety of healings, the forgiveness of every conceivable sin is difficult to comprehend. Is no one excluded from God's presence who approaches Jesus in faith to be healed? Is every believer blessed with the gift of new life in the kingdom of heaven? And Jesus discerns with the words of *wisdom*: "Blessed is the one who is not scandalized by Me" (Matt 11:6).

DISCERNMENT REGARDING KINGDOM

Jesus questions the crowds concerning their view of John the Baptist: "What did you go out into the wilderness to see?. . .a reed?. . .a man?. . .a prophet. . .?" (Matt 11:7-9). John the Baptist fulfills Israel's prophetic image as Elijah, the precursor of the Messiah, but Matthew adds a point of information for his community: "The little ones are greater than he (John the Baptist) in the kingdom of heaven" (Matt 11:11). Members of the community of Jesus' followers are called the little ones, the least, and the children of the kingdom of heaven (cf. Matt 10:43; 18:6, 10, 14).

The question of faith reassesses membership in the kingdom of heaven. There is a relationship between our expectations of the Messiah, the kingdom, and the meaning and interpretation we give to what is heard and seen.The kingdom was perceived as present by those who exercised force and violence in the execution and death of Jesus. These violent ones, the Gentiles, were able to discern the past and perceive the person of Jesus as the Messiah of the kingdom come. These violent ones take the kingdom by force (Matt 11:12f). The outcasts of society, the reprobate, are the people that Jesus invites. And the wisdom of God discerns: "The one who has ears to hear let that one hear (Matt 11:15).

DISCERNMENT REGARDING THIS GENERATION

Jesus offers his own discernment of the believers. What is this generation like? He compares this age of believers to children in the marketplace, perverse and obstinate playmates, who will not follow the rules of the game. This generation is as fickle as children who judge others on the basis of their own whims. "We piped to you, and you did not dance; we wailed, and you did not mourn" (Matt 11:17f). In Matthew's community situation there are ritual actions performed in different households—table fellowship or passover celebration. The forms of worship may differ but the goal of the liturgical action is the same. Should ritual action be judged on the basis of external forms or on the basis of the interior relationship in faith? God desires all to participate together at the banquet in the heavenly kingdom. Jesus gives no specific prescriptions on the external forms of the Law in the kingdom on earth.

In Matthew's community of believers, there were those who criticized Jesus and his followers for disregarding the laws of fasting during his public ministry, ". . .John came neither eating nor drinking, and they say, 'He has a demon' the Son of Man came eating and drinking, and they say, 'Behold, a glutton and a drunkard, a friend of tax collectors and sinners!' " (Matt 11:18f). Eating and drinking or not eating and drinking are arbitrary actions. It is the heart that interprets; it is the heart that sees. It is the heart that gives meaning to what we see and how we see with this interior perception in faith. And Jesus discerns: "Yet wisdom is justified by her deeds" (Matt 11:19).

Matthew is expressing in the words of Jesus the criticism that is leveled against Jesus, John the Baptist and their followers. They symbolize the old traditional observances as well as the new ritual celebration, which Jesus has come to offer to all who are able to hear. "Do this in remembrance of me" is a phrase that Matthew excluded from the Lord's Supper (Matt 26:28) but he has substituted the reminder that Jesus' blood is poured out for the forgiveness of sins. It is the purpose for which Jesus, the Christ, has come: to reveal God's continued presence with us, in life and in death. Jesus also ate with tax collectors and sinners. Jesus's action may give us pause as Christians, to re-evaluate how we see participation and membership at the table of the Lord.

The question of ritual practices reverts to the instruction given by Jesus in the Sermon on the Mount. To whom do we owe allegiance and for whom do we perform this duty of worship? (cf. Matt 6:1-18). Do we perform our actions before God in secret? Or do we perform our actions to be seen and thereby praised or judged by others? Our actions do receive payment in kind.

Does a person of faith judge another's action by his or her own personal answers? Does our question regarding the actions of another open us to more and more possibility for diverse answers? Equally as valuable are the insights and perceptions of others. They may be focusing and directing their actions toward the same goal (God). It gives us food for thought. Jesus discerns: "Blessed is the one who takes no offense (is not scandalized) at me" (Matt 11:6; 13:57).

DISCERNMENT IN PRAYER

The mighty works of God, the messianic deeds of healings, have been accomplished by Jesus; therefore the prophetic signs have been worked in Israel. Salvation has come to Israel. Prayerfully Jesus laments that in spite of so many prophetic acts of healing done in the cities, the people who saw the signs still did not repent. The ones who should have seen did not.

In prayer Jesus acknowledges his Fathers's good pleasure. He reveals the kingdom presence to children and hides it from the wise and the understanding (Matt 11:25-30). The Gentiles, those who did not know, are able to hear and understand. A discerning faith, the union of the divine and human wills, is able to respond, Yes! to God in prayer (Matt 11:26).

The word of *wisdom* invites: "Come to me all you who labor and are burdened and I will give you rest . . . learn from me" (Matt 11:28f). The demands of the Law are heavy but Jesus' burden is light.

In Jesus' prayer we see a need for praise and thanksgiving for all that is, for all that is in this world that makes life a blessing, for all the situations that prevent us from hearing and seeing the relationship of the person and the message of Jesus. The relationship of the Father and the Son is revealed to some and hidden from others. Yet this is all part of the kingdom and in this kingdom we pray that God's will be done on earth as it is in heaven (Matt 6:10).

But who are the children of God? Is Jesus offering the Gentiles a share in this relationship? Is Jesus in communion with the poor, the outcasts, the blind and those who believe in him? Is God one with those who are freed, liberated and saved from the Law by their faith in Jesus to cure, heal or forgive them?

For all that is, we give thanks and praise! The diversity that we experience in a faith existence need not cause division because it did not separate Jesus from those he loved, from those who followed, or from those who were intent on destroying him (Matt 13:53). In faith Jesus prays: "I thank you, Father, Lord of heaven and earth, that you have hidden these things from the wise and understanding and revealed them to babes" (Matt 11:25).

DISCERNMENT REGARDING THE LAW

The Pharisees approach Jesus regarding his disciples' observance of the Law. Jesus asks: How do you read and understand
the Law? What did David do? These questions deal with
aspects of temple, priesthood, and sabbath restrictions. They
relate to two contemporary images for discipleship in the
kingdom, interpretations that are both old and new. David
and those with him went into the *house of God*, a symbol which
is broader than the temple, and they ate the *Bread of Presence*,
another phrase that is symbol and sign of the eucharist. It was
also the sabbath, *a day set apart for the presence of the Lord* to be
reflected upon and experienced as the Lord's day. David and
those with him did what was not permitted to anyone but the
priests. They transgressed the Law in order to save their lives.
Faith asks: Were they guilty?

Jesus discerns with *wisdom* that the person is not a slave to
laws made by human beings. According to the standards of
God's Law, mercy has no restrictive days or hours. Time is
intended to serve the person. Faith encounters immediate
healing for the forgiveness of sin (Matt 9:13) and discerns: "I
desire mercy and not sacrifice" (Matt 12:7; 9:13).

Unity

The gift of healing or the forgiveness of sin was at the root of
the scandal that kept the community of believers from perceiving the kingdom (cf. Matt 11:6; 13:57). The community
could not see that God's mighty act of salvation in Jesus united
the individual with God, others, and the world. There is one
world only—the kingdom of heaven on earth. No one is

.excluded from the house of God. This kingdom is the world, the household of God which unites everyone to God in faith: those with different perceptions, different experiences, and different forms of worship. The kingdom symbol unites the heavenly realm with the earthly realm; both together are the place of the presence of God.

In Jesus God chooses to be united with humankind. He reveals God's desire to be one with creation and to create the world anew in raising up the Christ. There is nothing that separates God from this world, not even sin. Blasphemy against the Holy Spirit is the only deterrent in this age or at the close of the age (Matt 12:32). God shows the value of the human person in Jesus, who manifests and reveals the relationship of God with us. God chooses to reveal this unity of relationship to children (Matt 11:25-30).

The stories or parables of Jesus point to this worldly *and* heavenly reality. His presence touches every dimension of our life. This world is meant to be seen and experienced as the reign of God *now*.

WISDOM UNITES

The spirituality of the community is defined in the parables because they speak about an experience of faith that is personal and sacred to each individual. In the parable of the seed (Matt 13:1-23), the word of God touches the universal experience of all human beings living on the earth. All are able *to hear* the word of God. At the same time, the parable of the seed conveys that the realm of the heavenly is intimately bound up with what it means to be Christian and to be human. All human beings are able *to be* the word of God.

Wisdom's metaphorical imagery: "the kingdom of heaven is like . . ." allows the hearer to engage in the dialogic process and to question: "Am I like that?" In this manner of questioning, the old *promise* of salvation becomes ever new within the present context of the hearer.

SIN DIVIDES

Jesus speaks to us of God's perception of sin. The evils that are perpetrated in this world are not the will of God nor God's just judgment of evildoers. When our human acts do not coincide with the transcendent nature of our being, there is a rupture in that nature and a disruption in our relationship with God. This is what we call sin: to go against our true nature, to negate the divine element in our person that longs to express itself in our actions. We sever our relationships with God, self, and others by going against our basic human potential, which is created to serve both the human and the divine elements of our nature and this world. In this ordered world, nature has its own built-in rewards and punishments. Our actions have either the capacity to deform us as persons or the ability to transform us as human beings—in the kingdom.

There are times when our individual response, our action, the fruit of the seed (the word of God) is less than a hundredfold, less than full and complete, less than united with the will of God or *perfect.* There are times when as a community we produce little that will image the hundredfold or unity of the kingdom. There are times when we as individuals and as community are motivated to produce the hundredfold in the return of our gifts to God through our good and just deeds and words (Matt 12:33-37). There are times when the smallest of all seeds (the mustard seed) is able to grow in solitude and silence in our hearts and in our society. This smallest of seeds then becomes the true image that God presents to this world: the image of forgiveness and healing produces the flourishing tree where all types of birds flock. There are times when the yeast (teaching) leavens the whole mass of flour to extra-ordinary proportions and God's presence in the world is manifest. But it may also result in the individual and/or the community's becoming puffed up with self. There are times when the community scatters, or gathers together in utmost unity and harmony. There are times when we are caught up by faith into God; there are other times in our individual and communal lives when we are caught up in joy for a time, or choked by the cares of the world, or we are persecuted and burnt out. In the end of the age we will be judged on how we have allowed *the word of God* to inform and transform our lives—our world. How has our faith response served the *unity* of the kingdom of heaven on earth?

UNITY OF THE KINGDOM

The one seed, the word of God, growing within our different soils, is equally valuable for manifesting the mystery of the kingdom of heaven. All kinds of seeds and weeds, all types of fish, all manner of expressions and appearances are revelatory in this kingdom come (Matt 12:32; 13:40, 49). We ourselves pass judgment on our lives each day. At the close of the age, God will be the determining judge of our actions. For some there may be "weeping and gnashing of teeth" (Matt 13:42, 50; 8:12; 22:13; 24:51; 25:30). What better way to express utter frustration at the possibility of exclusion from the kingdom presence. Others may ask: "Where did this man get this wisdom and these mighty works?" (Matt 13:54). Indeed, the kingdom is both present and future; it includes all human beings, the violent (Gentiles) and the just (Jews). The opportunity exists for all peoples to be just and when the opportunity is seized, "The just shall shine like the sun in the kingdom of their Father" (Matt 13:9). The words of Jesus reverberate in our hearts and remind us: "But I say to you, Love your enemies, and pray for those who persecute you so that you may be children of your Father who is in heaven; for he makes the sun rise on the evil and on the good, and sends the rain on the just and on the unjust" (Matt 5:44f).

The children of this generation and the children of the kingdom reside together on earth. There is no apparent distinction between them. The encounter of healing and the unity of wills with God, the encounter with Jesus in faith, unites not only our actions but also our spirit with the Holy Spirit of God given to us in baptism. Jesus is the sign of this gift of a new life of resurrection. Jesus is the only sign given (Matt 12:38-42). This is John the Baptist's message. This is the same message Jesus has come to deliver as Messiah of the kingdom of heaven. Jesus' Spirit poured out upon the whole world enables everyone *to hear and to see.* This sign of God's presence is greater than the temple (the Law); greater than Jonah (the Prophet); greater than Solomon (the Wise man) (cf. Matt 12:6, 41f).

TO HEAR AND TO SEE

We are left free to discern and to decide for our life in this world: to believe in the power of God in Jesus to cast out demons, to heal, to forgive sins; or to be scandalized, which is to take offense at Jesus' actions. If the Spirit of God has cast out demons, then the kingdom of God has come upon us. If not, the kingdom, city, house, person will be divided (Matt 12:22-32). It requires faith to see the kingdom at hand. The word of God continues to be heard when we who have been commissioned to teach, preach, baptize, to give this same good news to the whole world, do so in Jesus' name and in his manner of forgiveness (cf. Matt 28:18-20). The word of God is the gift of forgiveness of sin to the world, and it is within our power to give forgiveness as children of the kingdom. A believer can take offense at Jesus by being scandalized that this power is given to human beings. But does not the gift of forgiveness also have the potential to create unity?

The word continues to be spoken in diverse historical and cultural conditions: "The one who has ears to hear, let that one hear" (Matt 11:15; 13:9, 43).

8

Presence:
The Fulfillment of Jesus' Expectations of Discipleship in the Kingdom (Matt 14-18)

Word/Way

At the time Matthew was writing, the Jewish Christian community was experiencing a strained relationship with Pharisaic Judaism because of its traditional religious observances. Although the Jewish Christian community still adhered to the mother faith, it had differing views regarding religious laws and ritual (to say nothing of its messianic claims about Jesus). This presented a conflict for the Jewish authorities and a conflict within the hearts of the believers who still desired to participate in the conventional religious practices.

The Law was central to the Pharisees' way of life. Because of this emphasis on *Law*, those committed to the *way of Jesus* probed more deeply into their Christian identity. If Jesus' teachings as interpreted in the Sermon on the Mount are normative for the Christian way of life, do the believers (Jewish Christians) have an obligation to observe the traditions that have been handed down by the elders? Are the ritual laws to be disregarded? What is the Christian identity in this world? Is the Christian way of life in continuity with the identity of the people Israel? Throughout the history of Israel, the people lived by faith in the promise of God. Now that the promise is fulfilled in Jesus, is the Christian way of life essentially different from the faith of Israel?

Matthew was deeply conscious that the Christian community, whether predominantly Jewish or Gentile, was in continuity with the renewed Israel. Undoubtedly, the twelve apostles who were called, named and sent (cf. Matt 10:1ff) symbolized continuity with the twelve tribes of Israel. Throughout the Gospel, Matthew stressed that Jesus, the fulfillment of the Scriptures, is/was consistent with Israel's expectations. And Matthew remarked that descendency from Abraham according to the flesh was not adequate; repentance was required (Matt 3:9). Obviously, the Jewish Christian community was aware of its continuity with Israel and its relationship to the person of Jesus, the Christ, who is also Emmanuel, "God-with-us" (Matt 1:23). These are but a few of the many traditional formulations in Matthew's Gospel that link the Christian heritage with Judaism. It is the aim of Matthew to point out the continuity of the Christian way of life with the way of Israel. To believe in God is to be in the presence of Jesus: this is *the way.*

Gradually, the term CHURCH (ekklesia) the Greek translation for the Hebrew word for assembly of people (Qahal), became the designation for those who were identified as the Christian community, both Jews and Gentiles. When the mixed community of Matthew's Church attempted to put Israel's renewed covenant commitment into practice in word and action/worship, apparently a conflict arose (Matt 16:18; 18:17).

Matthew utilized Jesus' encounters with the Jewish authorities to set forth strategically the teachings of the Sermon on the Mount for praxis. This enabled Matthew to engage the Church of his own day and Pharisaic Judaism in a dialogue. This led to the discernment of faith for praxis.

Jesus dialogues with religious leaders: Herod, the authority over the territory of Galilee (Matt 14:1-12); the Pharisees and Scribes responsible for ritual observances of the Torah (Matt 15:1-9); and the Pharisees and Sadducees, who kept a strict, uncompromising, conservative position regarding Torah as set down in the Book of Moses (Matt 16:1-4). In the persons of Peter and the disciples, Jesus dialogues with the leadership of the Church in Matthew's day (Matt 16:5-18: 35).

The persons who held religious leadership roles (Chapters 14-18) continued to doubt and fear and "test" Jesus' interpretation of the Law, which essentially elucidated an understanding of God. In a context of dialogue with Jesus, the word of God and the words of human beings came into tension. Matthew put Jesus in a situation of conflict with the religious authorities to show that the ultimate authority is GOD.

Persons in leadership roles were invested with certain powers by virtue of their office. They were to be trusted and held in honor and esteem by the society, be it civil, communal or religious. According to the code of relationships in the Ancient Near East, the people endowed them with ultimate earthly authority, and they neither questioned nor challenged their word or actions. Jesus broke this pattern by questioning them, indicating that he considered himself their peer.

POWER OF THE WORD

Herod, under Roman auspices, was ruler of the Jewish people. His word was law and it was not retractable. When Herod swore an oath, because he was indebted to Herodias' daughter (she pleased his guests by her dance), Herod could not recall his word of promise without losing fame, name, power. Though his position gave him a quasi-divine status, his honor was at stake. Even if it meant he would relinquish half his kingdom, he was bound to keep his word. Even though Herod disobeyed the commandments of God (by murder and adultery) as king, his word was held in honor. It could not be challenged by inferiors. Herod would be dishonored/defamed and powerless if he did not keep to the oath which he swore (Matt 14:9).

RESTRICTIONS OF THE WORD

The word of the Pharisees was the official and final word for many within Judaism. The Pharisees and Scribes had control over the observances of the Law and they interpreted the commandments of God by a multitude of significant or insignificant details. Legal jurisdiction included ritual washing of hands before eating and the laws regarding foods (Matt 15:2, 4, 20). Multiple practices were enforced in accord with their traditional customs. This was done in good faith to enhance characteristic observances of the Law. But it laid a great burden upon the people and at times became oppressive. It obscured the word of God. Jesus asks: "Why do you transgress the commandments of God for the sake of your traditions?" (Matt 15:3).

SIGNIFICANCE OF THE WORD

Jesus, the Teacher, challenged the Pharisees and Sadducees in
their quest for a sign from heaven (Matt 16:1, 5ff, 11; 3:7). In
their limited vision of the present world as the place for the
one encounter with God, they were unable to see in Jesus and
his precursor, John the Baptist, the true sign from heaven.
Jesus is the one person in whom THE direct encounter with
God takes place. The Sadducees knew that all of nature is a
sign that points beyond itself and speaks of another more
important reality: "You know how to interpret the appearances
of the sky but you know not how to interpret the signs of the
times" (Matt 16:3). It is the nature of the human person to
relate to God, to see God in the human condition. *In those days*,
the new age of Matthew's Church, a sign points to and speaks
of a time when life's meaning lies beyond, as well as in, the
present world: *in Jesus.*

AUTHORITY OF THE WORD

In the dialogue between Jesus and his disciples, Matthew's
Church receives an explanation of the community's questions
regarding a relationship to God. The traditions of the elders are
not disregarded but the legalization of customs and popular
ritual practices is to be avoided if they make void the commandment of God, the word of God (Matt 15:3, 6). God's
word, as spoken through the prophet Isaiah (29:13), is fulfilled
by the Pharisees: "This people honors me with their lips but
their heart is far from me; in vain do they worship me,
teaching as doctrines, the precepts of men" (Matt 15:9). The
word that proceeds from the heart may dishonor a person, not
ceremonial practices (Matt 15:11, 18, 20). Ritual actions that

become mandated as Law make void the commands of God—
the word of God (Matt 15:3, 6). God has placed commandments in the human heart to instruct and to teach what
concerns the relationship to God/self/others. Thoughts direct
action and proceed from the heart. The freedom to discern the
word of God and the freedom to choose the will of God
witness to the presence of God in the heart. This is obedience
to the commandments of God: this is the *way of Jesus.*

THE WORD OF THE WORLD AND
THE WAY OF JESUS

Leadership roles reflected the society in which Jesus lived.
Culture and custom dictated the ways in which the authoritative word and leadership functions were exercised. The way
of Jesus as the Law of God contrasted with the world's
perception and the world's response. Matthew's Church of
Jews and Gentiles was subject to two binding forces: the
natural law written on the heart, and ethnocentric beliefs
which may have had a tendency to be erratic.

For the Jews and the Gentiles, the way of Jesus is perceived
to be a word of WISDOM (Matt 13:54) and a prophetic action
(Matt 13:57; 14:2). The prophetic word bears the authority of
God but the question remains: "Where does this man get such
wisdom and these mighty works?" (Matt 13:54, 56). Matthew
advocates the way of Jesus and the word of Jesus for both Jews
and Gentiles. Is Jesus' action rooted in the authority of the
world or in the power of God?

The way of Jesus is compassionate, nourishing, life-giving,
enabling and supportive. The word of Jesus is bread for the
way in the wilderness of life (Matt 14:15-21; 15:32-39);
courage and peace in the panic of fear; and a word that saves

when the word rises from the heart (Matt 14:26-33).

The words of the world are capable of leading the blind astray and uprooting the seed (the word) planted in the heart of the believer (Matt 15:34f; 7:15-20). The words of the world are capable of tempting and leading the little ones into sin (Matt 18:5)); "Do not despise one of these little ones" (Matt 18:10f), or "lead one of these little ones who believe in me to sin" (Matt 18:6, 10f).

Jesus' way/word is capable of scandalizing the religious authorities (Matt 13:57; 15:12; 17:27; 18:6, 8; 5:29f), but it is also capable of seeking and saving the lost (Matt 18:12-14), of correcting faults (Matt 18:15-20) and forgiving sin (Matt 18:21f). Who are the ones who see and hear God in Jesus (Matt 17:1-9)? It is the disciples who glimpse the heavenly reality in the earthly realm and walk the way of Jesus in the midst of the ambiguity of this world. And as Peter testifies, these may be persons who deny Jesus (Matt 26:69-75) and return to the Lord in their sorrow to assume the mission of discipleship (Matt 28:18-20). But it is the little one, the child, whose heart is capable of beholding the face of God in heaven, who knows the need for God (Matt 18:2ff; 19:13ff).

Being in the presence of God's kingdom in this world transmits new life to both the traditional beliefs of Pharisaic Judaism and to Jewish Christianity. For the Church, a mixed community of Jews and Gentiles that commits itself to a relationship with God in Jesus, the authority of the word and the function of leadership in the community of believers reside in the person of *Jesus.* Jesus, Risen Lord and Spirit, given to the believers in a baptism of suffering, death and resurrection (Matt 16:21ff; 17:33f), creates a community of faith, hope and love. The code of God's wisdom, written Law, *resides* in the human heart. What makes it dynamic and living? *Faith* in

Jesus' word in action and worship that *proceed* from the human heart!

Fear/Faith

The Christian of Matthew's community stands in God's kingdom of heaven manifest here on earth. Jesus has shown by his word and his way, that being in the kingdom of heaven is *being in* the presence of God. Fear is the only obstacle to faith in Jesus, to hearing the word of God in the way of Jesus. Fear inhibits hearing the authority of the word in the heart and asks: "Where did this man get this WISDOM and these mighty works?" (Matt 13:54, 56). Fear results in Pharisaic Judaism taking offense, being embarrassed, disillusioned, unable to see and hear the power at work in Jesus and unable to choose the Jewish Christian community of Matthew's day. Faith requires relinquishing preconceptions; faith in Jesus requires surrendering previous ways.

FAITH

To *be in* the presence of God is faith. The house of David and the land of Judea were closed to the good news of the kingdom of heaven. Jesus replies: "A prophet is not without honor, except in his own country and in his own house" (Matt 13:57). These words apply specifically to Matthew's community of Jewish Christians, but they can apply to the Church in all times. The fear that blinds one from seeing the good in another limits the number of revelation moments: "He did not do *many* mighty works there because of their unbelief" (Matt 13:58). When faith is weak, forgiveness is less prevalent.

FEAR

The authoritative word of God in the word of John the Baptist caused terror in the heart of Herod, the ruling authority in Galilee: "It is not lawful for you to have her (Herodias, his brother Philip's wife)" (Matt 14:4). Herod had John the Baptist imprisoned. Distancing the one who is feared, banishing a person from one's territory, dismissing the one who is feared from one's presence, refusing to acknowledge another's word or action that may cause embarrassment and dishonor are all ways of dealing with fear. Denying the truth and goodness in another person is a way of coping with fear. It is also a way of denying life to another. Fear of hearing John the Baptist's word (the word of God) caused Herod to vow the death-dealing word. Herod lost the opportunity of encountering Jesus because, hearing about John, Jesus withdrew from that area (Matt 14:13).

FAITH/FEAR

The feeding of the multitudes (Matt 14:15-21; 15:32-39) evokes an image of Moses as Law-giver and provider of food for the journey of life. It also presents an image of Jesus as the presence of the word/way of God operative in Judaism. Because they had no provisions with them, the disciples were anxious and reluctant to face the crowds. "Send them (the people) away . . . to buy food for themselves" (Matt 14:15). Fear may surface as a lack of generosity and prevent sharing even what is available. Because the disciples failed to believe in the feeding of the multitudes (Matt 14:15), their faith was tested again. "Where are we to get enough bread in the desert . . .?" (Matt 15:33). Is this a lapse of memory or a lack of conviction in the power of Jesus? The Sermon on the Mount teaches: "Do not be anxious for your life" (Matt 7:25-33). There will always be sufficient for your needs. But such an attitude requires faith. To *be in* the presence of God overcomes fear and doubt concerning the past and gives confidence for the future.

Crossing over to the other side is a symbol of moving from Jewish Christianity to the Gentile world (Matt 14:22; 16:5). Did crossing over cause fear in the disciples? By prayer and discernment in faith at a time of transition, the Church asks: "Lord, if it is you, bid me come to you on the water" (Matt 14:28). Is the Gentile world also the reality of the presence of God? Is it possible to meet and encounter God in a realm that is foreign or in a people that do not know God? Peter and the disciples, representative of the leadership in the Church, overcome their fear of losing the former way of life with God by the Law. They open their eyes, hands and hearts to Jesus in their struggle to discern the word/way. In the midst of doubt and fear, Peter prays: "Lord, save me" (Matt 14:30). Fear is overcome even when faith is weak. "O ye of little faith, why do you doubt?" (Matt 14:31). The disciples acknowledge "God-with-us" in Jesus and confess: "Truly, you are the Son of God" (Matt 14:33). Faith—to be in the presence of God—overcomes fear and sees Jesus in the face of the other, whether Jew or Gentile. A magnificent example of this truth is illustrated in the brief incident: "And when they had crossed over, they came to land at Gennesaret. And when the men of that place recognized him (Jesus) they sent round to all that region and brought to him all that were sick, and besought him that they might only touch the fringe of his garment; and as many as touched it were made well" (Matt 14:34-36). This is Matthew's expression of forgiveness as healing, recognized and experienced in his own life and in the community of Church.

Fear of God is a positive and wholesome characteristic when rooted in the commandments of God. To be open to hear the word of God (the seed) planted in the soil of the human heart, it is necessary to listen, "to hear—and to understand" (Matt 15:10, 16). "For out of the heart come evil thoughts, murder, adultery, fornication, theft, false witness, slander" (Matt 15:19f). The Law of God written in the heart of all peoples confirms the just relationship with God, with self and with others. Fear of violating the rights of others can be wholesome and can reveal reverence and awe towards God. The one who receives another in my name receives me (Matt 18:5). And the whole Law is contained in the one commandment of LOVE: "Love God and your neighbor as yourself" (cf. Matt 22:38-40). Unwashed hands do not separate one from God, but the unclean heart will not be able to see God (Matt 15:20) as Matthew teaches through the Sermon on the Mount (Matt 6:22f).

FAITH WITHOUT FEAR

Faith is vicariously experienced by those from alien territory (Gentiles) who come to Jesus to be exorcised, healed or forgiven. All express the one reality of *being in* the presence of God.

The Canaanite woman (Matt 15:21f) asked Jesus to exorcise her daughter. "Have mercy on me, O Lord, son of David . . . Lord, help me" (Matt 15:22, 25). Contact with Gentiles implied ritual impurity for Judaism at the time of Jesus. The Church, in the persons of the disciples, those who knew their traditions, would have dismissed the woman. "Send her away . . ." (Matt 15:23). The woman's faith transcends the sin-boundaries of fear under Law, be it civil, communal or religious. She persists in appealing her case. Jesus replies: "Woman, great is your faith! Be it done for you as you desire!" (Matt 15:28). The bread of the children (the word of God) can also be given to the Gentiles in the kingdom of heaven on earth.

WEAK FAITH

A Church whose faith is weak does not perceive (Matt 14:25; 15:37), does not remember the teaching of Jesus (Matt 16:5-12). Weak faith is to be feared because it has the tendency to overlook the deeper realities of the way and the word of Jesus. It fails to recall or comprehend the words of Jesus regarding eucharist: "He blessed, broke, gave" the (Word), bread of Life to them to dispense to the multitudes without distinction; men, women and children. How many really yearn to be members of the kingdom! There was and is sufficient food for all!

FAITH IN THE WORD OF JESUS

The Church acknowledges Jesus as " . . . the Christ, the Son of the living God" (Matt 16:16; 22:22) who must go to Jerusalem, suffer many things from the elders, chief priests and scribes, be killed and be raised on the third day" (Matt 16:21-23).

The way of the world takes offense at the word of suffering. The way of Jesus embraces life in the kingdom; it embraces all of life as he goes on the way. By *being in* the presence of God, one is able to accept life with its manifold conflict situations. Even now, the boundaries of human nature are being transformed and transfigured in and through the life/death/resurrection of Jesus who has journeyed through the desert existence of life. Nourished by this word of God (as spoken in the heart) and supported by Jesus' life and example, life in time and history has meaning for those who learn the lesson of forgiveness, whether Jew or Gentile. When Jesus' life is perceived only as the redemption from and punishment for sin, one lives in fear. To *be in* faith effects a change of mind and heart, and a remembrance of God's faithfulness throughout history. God remembered the promise to Abraham in sending Jesus. God's faithful love in Jesus did not allow death to have power over life eternal (Matt 16:21-23; 17:22f). God did not punish Jesus. In God's plan Jesus was *handed over* to the human condition and the world made its choices in relationship to him. However, the Risen Lord has chosen to remain with the world all its days (Matt 28:20). In vain do human beings crucify themselves by doubt, memory and fear.

TO BE IN FAITH

Distress in times of suffering, apprehension and anxiety causes the forces of this world to impinge upon hope and love for the things of this world. To *be in* the presence of God, which is faith, does not lessen apprehension, anxiety, dread or fear. Suffering and death are mysteries of life. Although suffering and death are inconsistent with a perception of life in the kingdom, they seem to be in continuity with the way of the prophets, the way and the word of Jesus. Indeed, the Law and the Prophets are fulfilled! To be a believer means to *be in* the presence of Jesus in life through death which is eternal life begun. It is a difficult word to comprehend, but faith overcomes fear.

TO BE IN THE WAY

Suffering is integral to discipleship (Matt 16:24-28; 28:18-20). Jesus testified to this by word and example. How fitting it is that the mystery of the transfigured glory-image of God in Jesus confirms Jesus as Son of God. Jesus has gone before us to show us the way. Faith-filled fear acknowledges with awe and reverence, "It is good for us to be here" (Matt 17:5f). And the word of the Father declared: "This is my beloved Son in whom I am well pleased; listen to him" (Matt 17:5).

The man with the epileptic son acknowledged Jesus by asking mercy on his son who suffered terribly (Matt 17:15). The disciples could not cure or exorcise the devil. Here the disciples are typified as the faithless, perverse generation: "How long am I *to be with* you; how long am I to bear with you?" (Matt 17:17). Jesus came to save Israel from her sin. God's forgiveness and love are continued in the present as the word of God and the way of God in Jesus. This is the Christian identity. A life in faith witnesses to the reconciling love of God for all humankind. Fear is great, but faith can be as small as a grain of mustard seed. Nothing would be impossible with faith (Matt 17:21); even the littlest of faith. Still faith and fear walk hand-in-hand!

9

Presence:
The Fulfillment of End-Time
Expectations of the Kingdom
(Matt 19-25)

Relationships

Matthew continued to instruct the leaders of his Church of Jewish and Gentile believers concerning value judgments placed upon one's relationships in this world. Jesus summarized the Law of God as one command under two aspects:

> "You shall love the Lord your God with all your heart, and with all your soul, and with all your mind. This is the great and first commandment. And a second is like it. You shall love your neighbor as yourself. On these two commandments depend all the law and the prophets." (Matt 22:37-40)

Jesus, the Teacher, reminds Israel of the value God places on relationships in the kingdom where the fulfillment of the Law derives from the one Law of love. *To do* and *teach* justice fulfills the one Law of LOVE and requires a ministry of forgiveness. Undoubtedly, Matthew has comprehended the profundity and the simplicity of the message. Israel's basic relationship to

God has not changed. A new understanding and the exercise of this new relationship with God in and through apparently ordinary, everyday routine interactions with others, fulfill the Law and the Prophets. This is the demonstration of the reciprocal relationship of God's love for humankind.

Does this one relationship of love include the Gentiles also? Jesus offers a reversal of the model of interpretation that dictates external observances. He suggests the inversion of human values from the external to the internal realm and prescribes the reversal from the divine to the human realm of practice. Matthew presents this message in the scene of the end-time judgment and offers insights into kingdom relationships by means of the dialogue between Jesus (the king) and his followers (Matt 24-25). One is worthy of membership in the kingdom of heaven when true human relationships for God are valued and lived in the kingdom on earth.

A radical reversal of religious practices and the inverse structure in human relationship could not be accepted even in faith unless Jesus had passed this way as witness to God's Word and as exemplar of human values. In chapters 21-25, Jesus continues on the way to Jerusalem and sets his followers on the path to freedom where the judgments of the world and the judgments of God come into conflict or tension. Christian discipleship moves continually in the inverse direction of this ONE relationship. The service we render to God proceeds from the heart: from oneself, through the other to God and demonstrates the ONE LOVE, the ONE COMMANDMENT (Matt 22:40). True love of the other can only proceed from a true love of self that proceeds from the true love of the heart— Who is God.

Although Jesus had given his interpretation of the Law and the Prophets in the Sermon on the Mount, questions regarding the application of the Law and the Prophets continued to be "tested" by the authorities within Judaism. Matthew reiterates Jesus' teaching by using the three familiar modes of instruction: the question and answer form of the authorities; the parabolic metaphors of kingdom images; and the great discourse or sermon of Jesus couched in the scene of the so-called last judgment. The questions and answers, the parables and the discourse deal with different aspects of the one relationship in the kingdom.

The specific questions addressed to Jesus in chapters 19-22 by the Pharisees concern the Jewish Christian observances of the Mosaic Law in matters of relationship in marriage and views regarding celibacy (Matt 19:3-12). The Herodians were concerned about the tax paid to the Roman government by the Jewish Christians in Matthew's day, since Pharisaic Judaism was exempt from the tax as it had been in Jesus' day. What, therefore, is the Church's relationship to civil authorities and what type of allegiance do Christians owe to Caesar (Matt 22:15-22)? The Sadducees disagreed with the Pharisees regarding the doctrine of the after-life, and Matthew sought Jesus the Teacher's affirmation regarding resurrection faith because Jesus is now proclaimed as Lord, Risen from the dead (Matt 22:23-33). The legal question posed by the Lawyers challenged the community and Jesus' understanding of the Great Commandment of the Torah (Matt 22:34-40). These questions concerned disputes raised by the Jewish synagogue leaders of Matthew's day as well as all those issues specifically related to the community's relationship with God and its relationship to others.

Matthew emphasizes the ONE relationship in the kingdom of heaven. God, others and oneself are intrinsically bound together in Jesus, "God-with-us." This gift of God's presence within the human person is the mystery inherent in Christian faith. In today's world this is called the life of grace or the graced existence. In the time of Jesus it was known as God's presence (WISDOM) incarnate in the world.

Jesus gives a message of unity and community of all humankind for all time. The kingdom is ONE, the people of God are ONE, and the time is ONE, now and forever. This ONE gospel message resounds throughout the multiple pedagogical forms used by Jesus. Matthew relates incidents in the life of Jesus to depict *those days* as the time of the kingdom. Now that *those days* have arrived, there is only one PLACE: God's presence is the kingdom come.

ONE RELATIONSHIP OF PLACE IN THE KINGDOM

Jesus approached the CITY of Jerusalem, his own city, and was identified by the crowds and by the children as son of David (Matt 21:9). The king entered his own city on the humble beast of burden, and thus fulfilled the prophecies of Zechariah and Isaiah: "Tell the daughter of Zion, behold, your king is coming to you, humble, and mounted on an ass, and on a colt, the foal of an ass" (Matt 21:5; Isa 62:11; Zech 9:9). Jesus was acclaimed by the simple and the humble folk as the MESSIAH, the one who comes in the Name of the Lord! Jesus, the Lord, entered his holy city and was received by the little ones. Children have few investments in the temporalities of *land*, or *house*, and recognize Jesus—their king and Lord. For children, the relationship with the *person* of Jesus far exceeds the values of all other realms and external appearances. The human person is the place of encounter with God.

The TEMPLE in the holy city of Jerusalem was a place of worship and prayer (Matt 21:12f). In Jesus' day the House of

God was engaged in plea-bargaining for the support of ritual practices that were equated with or interpreted as the way to an encounter with God. The buyers and sellers endeavored to transact heavenly gains with worldly interest. But God resides and is recognized in the heart of the ones who are meek and humble. The heart is the true place of worship and the place where one engages in a dialogue of faith and prayer. The dutiful moneymongers and grasping peddlers do violence to the value of the human person by robbing the attention of one's heart: the place of union and prayer. The heart is the place where personal needs can be known and revealed. Jesus' action of cleansing the temple gives a message. Not only is the place, the physical domain violated, the place in the heart is also torn and divided by the exchange of monetary goods for spiritual benefits. Matthew, like Jesus, was adamant about the ONE place of worship and prayer—the heart of the human temple. The human heart is the place of encounter with God. "Out of the mouth of babes and sucklings thou hast brought perfect praise" (Matt 21:16; Ps 8:2).

The heart and mind of the little ones, the children, the blind and the lame are the CITY, TEMPLE, and LAND where God dwells (Matt 21:14f). God's relationship in the heart of all peoples is the new place of presence. The place of the Holy One is the dwelling place in the mind and heart of all those who know that they are loved, have needs, and encounter Jesus in the "other." The "other" is recognized as the "self" in the heart of the meek and the lowly. There is an identification of relationship. The "other" is the place where we encounter God.

The question of position and place at the right and the left side of Jesus in the kingdom is reserved for the ones whom the Father appoints (Matt 20:20-28). Matthew reminds the community that the ones who have a place in the kingdom of heaven are those who give of themselves to the suffering human condition as Jesus did, and become servants of all (Matt 20:17-20). "You know that the rulers of the Gentiles lord it over them, and their great men exercise authority over them. It shall not be so among you; but whoever would be great among you must be your servant, and whoever would be first among you must be your servant; even as the Son of Man came not to be served but to serve, and to give his life as a ransom for many" (Matt 20:25-28).

ONE RELATIONSHIP OF TIME IN THE KINGDOM

Time is ONE in the presence of God. There is no past, present or future with God. Whenever and wherever one resides *in those days*, is the opportune TIME of God's presence. Whether one enters the vineyard of the Lord's service at the beginning or the close of the day (in history), there is but ONE priority; to realize the present moment as the time of God's presence. The invitation to encounter God is promised to all peoples for all time by the Father of Jesus (Matt 20:1-16). And God gives what is JUST. God's choice, generosity and justice is ONE throughout all ages; the ONE gift of love is the same; the judgments that we make on the length of time of service are not a value in the judgment of God. The last shall be as the first and the first may even be the last to enter into the kingdom of heaven (the presence of God here on earth) (Matt 19:30; 20:16). The priority of *time* and the priority of *place* have no significance in the presence of God: God is ONE.

Time is not of the essence in Matthew's message of the spirituality of Jesus. The purpose of time is to give one the opportunity to achieve the goal of all judgment and that is: to make decisions in the light of what it means to be "with God." We experience God's presence here and hereafter by choosing God's will, the (LAW), God's PEACE (JUSTICE AND MERCY) and God's FAITH in us (Matt 23:23). It behooves us not to neglect these weightier matters! *In those days* defies chronological calculation. "Am I not allowed to do what I choose with what belongs to me? Or do you begrudge my generosity?" (Matt 20:15).

ONE RELATIONSHIP OF PERSONS IN THE KINGDOM

Jews and Gentiles, symbolic of all peoples who see themselves as separate and special in the plan of God, are reminded that they are ONE in the kingdom of heaven.

The external observances of the Law are not in accord with God's perception. God created male and female but they are joined in marriage in the ONE relationship of union; the two become one flesh (Matt 19:5). For this reason, "What God has joined together let no one put asunder" (Matt 19:6). Love, the principle in life and action, is God's creative gift. The external letter of the Law or the Mosaic commands focus on the uniformity of the command and its observances. Without the other's best interests at heart, without the union of mind and heart with God, the Law profits nothing.

The ones who have faith in the presence of the kingdom continue to pray; they do not doubt and consequently, are able to see the presence of the kingdom (Matt 21:18-22). The tax collectors and harlots approach Jesus as people who desire forgiveness and seek wholeness (Matt 21:31). These are welcomed into the kingdom. The children of Israel are like two sons who go into the vineyard. One son promises to serve in the kingdom but does not. The other son refuses to serve but has a change of mind and heart, and serves. "Which of the two did the will of his Father?" (Matt 21:31). The people (Israel) who plead ignorance, who "do not know" or refuse to accept Jesus' authority, his mighty deeds and honor, fail to see the presence of God. Producing fruit for the kingdom is salvation. Who produces the fruit of the kingdom? "The kingdom of God will be taken away from you and given to a nation producing the fruits of it" (Matt 21:43). Wisdom's parabolic teaching serves as a warning for all peoples.

There is one relationship within the kingdom. Both adults and children have equal membership in the household of God (Matt 19:13-15). The least are as the greatest in the ONE relationship within the kingdom, the family of God (Matt 18:1-4). "The ones who have followed . . . the ones who have left HOUSE, FAMILY, LAND will inherit eternal life" (Matt 19:29). This description seems to fit Jews as well as Gentiles: all peoples for all time.

With Matthew the basic issue is relationships. Time or place have validity and value only to the extent that they are given meaning by the person. How time and place affect the whole of personal relationships is the sole criterion of judgment. The person is the absolute; the person is the goal, the end and the value of all human relationships offered in love and in service.

A truly loving human experience is possible only when it is expressed, completed and incarnated in a human person. Every human heart and every area of life involves relationships which affect the possibility of growth at every stage of a person's life. Full human realization is possible only when love and duty, compassion and forgiveness are enshrined in the human encounter. We relate as true disciples to the "other" when we are present as "God-with-us" at the time and in the place of the other's need. This just relationship is an act of worship of God for it reflects Jesus' concept of the person: ultimately worthy, unique and clothed in mystery. Every life situation is in fact a relationship situation. The processes and the struggles involved in establishing just relationships in every time and place are the stuff of which love and life are made and are in fact, the kingdom of God with us.

Judgments

WHAT JUDGMENTS DO WE IMPOSE UPON GOD, OTHERS, SELF?

The parables give us an insight into God-likeness. God is like a father-king who invited guests to the marriage of his son (Matt 22:1-14). The invited guests (Israel) refused to come to the feast. The servants (prophets) went to the highways and streets and gathered all those they found. The ones who are called are judged worthy of the identity of the kingdom by their response. The baptismal robe of innocence is the sign of the relationship with Father and Son as participating member in the banquet of eternal life. Not the external signs of rites and rituals but the internal robe of just response is deemed worthy by God. God does not judge by human standards of judgment. God is persistent father/king/judge of all.

The justice due to God is different from the justice expected by the rulers of this world. The two orders of governance are in harmony and in relationship in the kingdom of this world. They are not competing powers since tribute is due to both powers in their differing realms. We live in ONE WORLD with visible and invisible powers. Choose whom you wish to serve! (Matt 22:15-22; 6:24). As servants of the ONE Master (Christ) we cannot give our allegiance to two lords (God/World) or competing rulers. What we do to God is done in service to the "other." The world is God's realm of action and our realm of service. God is not a ruler competing for the world. "All the tithe of the land, whether of the seed of the land or the fruit of the trees is the Lord's; it is holy to the Lord" (Lev 27:30).

Jesus teaches the Word of God, the Way of God truthfully. Jesus does not regard the position of human beings (Matt 22:16). He treats all human beings as ONE under God. Relationships in the kingdom of heaven are not determined as we determine relationships on earth. The levirate marriage laws do not apply in the kingdom of heaven. The relationships in the kingdom are not judged by the standards of human perception. And it is Jesus who judges others as ourselves, in the moment of revelation and truth (Matt 25:31-46).

The great commandment of God: Love of God and of neighbor as self is the message for all time. There is ONE TEACHER, Jesus; there is ONE FATHER, God; there is ONE MASTER, Christ. We are all brothers and sisters in the ONE KINGDOM of heaven (Matt 23:8-10).

The kingdom will be taken from a nation (Israel) and given to another nation producing FRUIT: just deeds are the all important response in the kingdom of heaven (Matt 21:44). The fruit of a good life is to do what is JUST. Once again, this is God's Wisdom.

WHAT JUDGMENTS DO WE MAKE ON OTHERS?

The activity for the kingdom presence is invested in Law,

justice, mercy and faith (Matt 23:23). The hypocrite or play-actor is concerned about the external image. The word responds to what is seen. God is concerned about the internal desires of the heart because the heart is the place where self encounters God. The heart is the mission territory where Christian ministry begins. The mind of the person, the place of the heart, and the interior vision can be closed to the presence of God. A person may swear by oath because the words have no depth. They speak what is right but they do not DO what is JUST. The indictment of the Pharisees may be the indictment of any Church leader or membership: "Do what they tell you but not what they DO! They preach and do not practice" (Matt 23:3). Matthew reminds the community *in those days.*

Essential religion is this: Do justice, keep the Law (of the heart) and practice mercy in faith. Faith which keeps the Law of the heart, the word of God, ever before the mind's eye will do justice as it relates to God/others/oneself. To be in the END-TIME and to come into judgment with the Lord at any time, is religion and the privilege of being Christian. Is there a weightier matter of the Law (Matt 23:23)?

The signs of the coming of the close of the age or the END are near (Matt 24:13f). When love has grown cold, when the question of salvation rises, when the forgiveness is no longer given as the gift received, then God will enter into judgment with the human condition. The ONE LAW of God's justice is LOVE and the one Law can be utilized in all aspects and ways of life. In the midst of apostasy, persecution, death and wars, there is still the ability to exercise LOVE—when all other ministries cease: the gospel of the kingdom (God's presence with us) will be preached throughout the WORLD as a witness to all nations . . . and then the end will come (Matt 24:13f). Love is the only remaining criterion of judgment and it lies in the human heart. The faithful servants will be as the stewards of the household of God who give food (the Word) at the proper time. They will keep faith; they will not let the enemy, unforgiveness, enter into the sole place of refuge, the heart. And the ones to be saved will give LOVE to the other as they give love to themselves. The message of love parallels the message of forgiveness: Forgive us as we forgive others! Love us as we love others! What an awesome prayer and what an extreme position for judgment; the so-called last judgment. It is the terminal point of our life and death experience, and it happens daily.

THE JUDGMENT ON THE SELF IS FOREBODING

The wisdom of God calls out: Be attentive—watch, be ready, be prepared to meet the bridegroom when he comes (Matt 25:1-13). The ONE commandment of love is to be exercised at all times. Some will be prepared and some will not; some will be wise and some will be foolish (Matt 25:8). Wisdom invites one to receive the gifts of life and to use the gifts, the talents that are given for this ONE WORLD. The gifts are to be acknowledged and used as the gifts that God gives. The one whom *wisdom* acknowledges will enter into the joy and happiness of the kingdom presence even NOW.

The good and faithful servant exercises the gifts and uses the talents (Matt 25:14-30). Forgiveness is the gift given to enable the community to exercise the oneness of being: GOOD, as God created the world to be. The wicked and slothful servant hides and preserves the gift for safekeeping. The TIME that is our lifetime is meant to be a time when gifts are multiplied and used in the service of the neighbor. Blessing and curse in the kingdom of heaven on earth result from the joy or the fear of the "other."

The inversion of the kingdom values and the world's values are demonstrated in the judgment scene: to do to God—first do to others, and what is done to others will be done to God. The reward and the curse are dependent upon the deeds that are done to the least of the brothers and sisters. Wisdom invites: COME! Blessed of my Father, and possess the kingdom that is prepared from the foundation of the world (Matt 25:46). The kingdom perception is always a question of discernment: When did we see you? The eye of the body is deceptive. The eye of the mind and heart perceives the inner dimensions where in the midst of serving another the heart "sees" and "hears" the invitation, "COME!"

God invites those who are transformed from within; those who receive a change of mind and heart as the gift of new life; those who recognize the gift, the beatitude of a new life in relationships with the poor, the lame, the dispossessed and the persecuted. Those who are blessed with the experience of new life in the kingdom have already related to God in the hungry, the thirsty, those imprisoned in earthly or despicable conditions. The ones who celebrate with the true, the beautiful and the good that this world offers are blessed as well. The gift that God gives is forgiveness of sin and IN THOSE DAYS ushers in the era of blessing and happiness. The ones whom Jesus forgave in his healing ministry, the ones who recognize Jesus and discern unity in the incomprehensible situations of this world, these are the ones who are blessed. The ones who carry on the mission of forgiveness in the footsteps of Jesus (on earth) and have served the will of God (in heaven) celebrate the ONE relationship that Jesus taught as the PRAYER for all time: the OUR FATHER. The ones who are able to pass from earthly life to life eternal on the day of judgment (every day) when the fulfillment of the goal has been reached will have related to the "other" as oneself. Then the members will participate with the fullness of vision and see God's life and light eternally. And these are the ones Wisdom judges blessed!

10

Presence:
The Fulfillment of the Expectations
of the Promise to the World
(Matt 26-28)

Decisions to Hand on the Message

From its inception, the Church has been designated a missionary Church. Beginning with the apostolic period, a missionary effort has been directed toward the Gentile nations. St. Paul and the Hellenists were known for their proselytizing activity among the Gentiles of Asia Minor and beyond. However, in Jesus' lifetime and in the historical situation in which Matthew was writing, missionary activity was concentrated on the proclamation of the gospel to the Jews who became the first Jewish Christians.

It is presumed that Jesus did not expect a mission to the Gentiles: "Do not go in the way of the nations, and do not enter the Samaritan cities" (Matt 10:5f; 15:24). But it is also stated in Matthew's Gospel that the community of disciples expected the kingdom to be preached to the whole world before the end of time (Matt 24:14; 26:13). Undoubtedly, the missionary endeavor to make disciples of all peoples has come about in fulfillment of the commission of Jesus in his risen ministry as the Christ: "All authority has been given to me in heaven and upon earth. Going, therefore, make disciples of all nations, baptizing them in the name of the Father and of the Son and of the Holy Spirit; teaching them to hold fast to all that I have commanded you. And behold, I am with you all days, until the end of the age" (Matt 28:18b-20).

At the time of Matthew's writing, this shift has taken place. Not only is the mission effort directed to the Gentiles but the specific ministry of Jesus, to teach and to evangelize, has also been mandated to the disciples. Throughout the Gospel, the disciples are commissioned to heal, to cast out demons and to announce the good news of the kingdom among the lost sheep of Israel (Matt 10:1, 5f; 12:18, 21), It is only at the end of Matthew's Gospel that the final commission to teach, the prerogative that rested with Jesus alone, was mandated as the future apostolic mission.

The prophet Isaiah had revealed God's will that the Messiah "...shall proclaim justice to the Gentiles ... and in his name will the Gentiles hope" (Matt 12:18, 21). That all nations would be disciples of Jesus is consistent with the prophetic word. In continuity with the first century community of believers and despite the inconsistencies we face in today's world, this faith-decision to hand on the message rests with us.

Chapters 26-28 focus on scenes that actualize the faith decisions of Jesus, of his followers, the communities of Jews and Gentiles, and of the crowds. Jesus is presented as a prophetic figure who predicts the events of his passion and death. "You know that after two days the Passover is coming, and the Son of Man will be handed over to be crucified" (Matt 26:2). This is not only a prophetic, authoritative decision. It presumes a decision that is made in obedience to the will of his Father according to the Scriptures (Matt 26:15, 31, 64; 27:9, 34, 43, 46).

Prophetic utterance is a traditional way of speaking about the word of God addressed to Israel of old. A person who is totally committed to the will of God in spirit and life, who is one with God in believing, hoping, loving, validates this predictive expression. This person is, indeed, a prophet. But Jesus is more than a prophet. In Jesus, the message and the person are one. To hear and see the good news proclaimed in the events of the life, death and resurrection of Jesus manifests a visible sign of the continuing presence of "God-with-us." In terms of universal mission, to *hand on* the message is to *hand over* the person of the risen Lord as he has commissioned us (Matt 28:20).

PROPHETIC WORD (Matt 26:1-27:26)

The predictive voice of Jesus enhances the events of his time of deliverance. "But all this has taken place that the Scriptures of the prophets might be fulfilled" (Matt 26:56). These narrative events characterize God's willingness to be *handed over* to the human condition from birth to death. *Handing over* is key to the mystery of Jesus' life and death. It epitomizes the progressive unfolding of the passion and death of Jesus. Jesus predicts that the Son of Man will be *handed over* to be crucified (Matt 26:2) and announces the hour when the Son of Man will be *handed over* to sinners (Matt 26:45b). Jesus is *handed over* by Judas (Matt 26:15f) to the Sanhedrin (Matt 26:57), to Pilate (Matt 27:2), to the will of the people (Matt 27:20-22), and to the soldiers for execution and death (Matt 27:26).

It is never said that Jesus is given over to death; Jesus willingly *hands over* his life, his body, his Spirit to his Father. Jesus is in control of his life, specifically, in death.

Handing over involves a conscious determinative act. Active participation in the process of *handing over* or *handing on* is an outward expression of an internal decision. The passion narrative demonstrates a form of deliverance governed by religious and/or political factors. The choice and decision for Jesus' crucifixion and subsequent death was a judgment made by political authorities for political reasons based on religious language symbols. In Matthew's Gospel, Jesus is *handed over* because of the accusation of blasphemy. His claim to be the Christ (Matt 26:64) and his claim to be the Son of God (Matt 27:11, 40, 43) gave Pilate, the political ruler, no right to judge this man on these religious charges. Recognizing Jesus' innocence, Pilate had no legal grounds for condemning him. Therefore, ironically, he turns to the people and submits his decision to their will: "What do you think?" (Matt 26:66). The people's verdict was "Crucify him!" (Matt 27:22f).

Decisions to Hand Over Jesus

Matthew offers insights into the decisive moments of *handing over* Jesus in the detailed account of the Passion. It is beneficial for us to concentrate on the decisions and the interpretations that are given for the actions of the 'dramatis personae.' They are typical of us all.

DECISIONS IN DIALOGUE (Matt 26:1-16)

The chief priests and elders of the people gather in the palace of Caiaphas, the High Priest, and make their decision. They conspire to arrest Jesus, take him by stealth and kill him. However, it is the time of the feast and the people may revolt. Since he has a great following, there may be a tumult among the people. Nonetheless, their decision is made: his type of kingdom must come to an end. This is not a new plan; it is the termination of a plot. "When the chief priests and Pharisees heard his parables, they tried to arrest him but they feared the multitude because they held him to be a prophet" (Matt 21:46).

This scene is followed by a decision of Jesus. He accepts the invitation to a meal in the house of Simon, designated the leper, a person characterized as a sinner. While at table a woman anoints the head of Jesus with expensive nard. The head is a symbol of power and authority in the Mediterranean world. Her action could be interpreted as a sign of her acceptance of Jesus as Lord of her life. The disciples focus on the woman who performs her action in view of all. In their indignation they suggest an alternative action: "Why this waste? This ointment might have been sold for a large sum and the money given to the poor" (Matt 26:9).

Jesus bestows life-giving meaning on the negative interpretation of the disciples. Jesus appropriates this anointing as a service done to him in preparation for his burial. The past act has present meaning and future purpose. The prophetic word of Jesus proclaims the woman's deed as an historical, universal memorial of her.

JESUS' DECISION AND DIALOGUE OF BETRAYAL (Matt 26:17-29)

It was after the Passover meal, the Jewish ritual remembrance of Israel's deliverance, that Jesus was delivered into their hands. "My time is at hand, I will keep the Passover at your house with my disciples" (Matt 26:18b-19). He predicts the hour and the person who will betray him to the Jewish and the Gentile authorities.

Judas himself admits to his action by a question: "Is it I, Master?" Jesus confirms the decision of Judas. "You have said so!" (Matt 26:25b). Jesus makes no judgment.

The *handing over* of life through death is announced in the Passover meal and a new interpretation is given to the festival celebration. The bread and wine becomes for them his body and blood. The new covenant is poured out for many for the forgiveness of sins. This predictive word of Jesus reflects the Isaian prophecy of the sacrifice of the suffering servant for the redemption of the many. This new covenant in Jesus' blood is to make definitive, once-for-all, the relationship of "God-with-us."

This is the memorial that he has left us, the sign of his presence with us for all time. The significance of the *handing over* of life through death is the life-giving presence that Christians celebrate in the Eucharistic meal as a remembrance of Jesus. The forgiveness of sins is the gift and the fruit of the covenant, a new life that will be lived eternally "in my Father's kingdom" (Matt 26:29).

DISCIPLES' DECISION (Matt 26:30-35)

"Even if I must die with you I will never deny you. And so said all the disciples" (Matt 26:34, 35). Peter's denial and the disciples' desertion are decisions with only temporary effects. Jesus assures the disciples of his resurrection, his shepherding of the flock, his leadership of the community in Galilee after the resurrection. Peter denies the Lord three times and the disciples abandon Jesus and flee (Matt 26:56b, 69-75). But all the Scriptures of the prophets must be fulfilled (Matt 26:56a).

JESUS' DECISION IN PRAYER (Matt 26:36-44)

The place is Gethsemane; the disciples wait; Peter and the two sons of Zebedee remain with Jesus at his bidding "to watch and pray." His prayer is one of deliverance from suffering and yet his ultimate decision is that the will of his Father be done (Matt 26:39, 42, 44).

JESUS' DECISION IN DIALOGUE WITH THE DISCIPLES (Matt 26:45-56)

"Behold, the hour is at hand and the Son of Man is betrayed into the hands of sinners. Rise, let us be going; see, my betrayer is at hand" (Matt 26:45f). Jesus willingly submits to the familial kiss of Judas that identifies him as "the man." One of the disciples draws a sword to protect Jesus. A decision of violence is self-destructive. "If you use the sword you will perish by the sword" (Matt 26:52). Jesus' response is provocative. It reiterates the teaching of the Sermon on the Mount: "Whatever you wish that others should do to you, do so to them, for this is the Law and the Prophets" (Matt 7:12).

Peter's denial was threefold: Peter denied being with Jesus by evading the question, "I don't know what you mean" (Matt 26:70). He denied with an oath that he even knew Jesus. The third was an accusation made against Peter himself: "Certainly you are also one of them; your accent betrays you" (Matt 26:73). But Peter began to curse himself and to swear: "I do not know the man" (Matt 26:72).

Judas, the betrayer, repented and confessed, "I have sinned in betraying innocent blood!" The chief priests and the elders replied, "What is that to us?" Judas took action against himself. He went out and hanged himself (Matt 27:5), whereas Peter went out and wept bitterly (Matt 26:75).

DECISIONS IN DIALOGUE WITH THE SANHEDRIN (Matt 26:57-68)

The scribes and the elders had gathered at the palace of Caiaphas, the high priest (cf. Matt 26:2) while Peter followed at a distance to see the end. The chief priests and the whole council sought for FALSE testimony against Jesus, that they might put him to death. Their testimony against Jesus was his claim to be the Christ, the Son of God. In their minds this was blasphemy, whereas in reality, Jesus is the Christ, the Son of God. The council *hands over* its decision to the crowd: "What do you think?" (Matt 26:66). The crowd responds with the decision that he deserves death. The crowd ridicules and mocks Jesus. They spit in his face, they strike him and slap him saying: "Prophesy to us, you Christ! Who is it that struck you?" The Sanhedrin, therefore, took counsel against Jesus to put him to death. They bound him and led him away and *handed him over* to Pilate the Governor.

DECISION OF THE ROMAN GOVERNOR
(Matt 27:11-26)

Pilate knew that it was out of envy that the chief priests and the elders *handed Jesus over* for judgment. Pilate's wife, a Gentile woman, made her decision in response to a dream: "Have nothing to do with that JUST man" (Matt 27:19), a response not too unlike the Gentile sages of the Infancy narrative. Undoubtedly, this man is "of God"—a JUST MAN.

Pilate had decided to release Jesus called Christ. The chief priests and elders persuaded the people to ask for Barabbas. When Pilate saw he was gaining nothing and the force of his decision was waning, he took water and washed his hands, an Old Testament symbol (Dt 21:6-9). This was followed by further rejection reflected in the cry of all the people: "His blood be on us and on our children" (Matt 27:25).

DECISIONS OF THE SOLDIERS OF THE GOVERNOR
(Matt 27:27-31)

The soldiers gathered the whole battalion, stripped Jesus, put a scarlet robe upon him, plaited a crown of thorns, put it upon his head, put a reed in his right hand and kneeling before him mocked him: "Hail, King of the Jews!" (Matt 27:29). They spat upon him, took the reed and struck him on the head. When they mocked him, they stripped him of the scarlet robe and put his own clothes on him. Then they led him away to crucify him.

They compelled Simon a man from Cyrene, a city of North Africa, to carry his cross. Over his head they put the charge against him: "This is Jesus, the King of the Jews" (Matt 27:37). The chief priests, scribes and elders mocked him saying: "He is the king of Israel. Let him come down NOW from the cross and we will believe in him. He trusted in God; let God rescue him NOW if he desires him, for he said: I AM THE SON OF GOD" (Matt 27:43).

The robbers crucified on his right and left side reviled him in the same way.

DECISION OF JESUS TO QUESTION GOD
(Matt 27:45-50)

In prayer on the cross Jesus offers the invocation of Psalm 22:1: "My God, my God, why have you forsaken me?" (Matt 27:46). His decision always to do the will of his Father remained firm until the very end of his life on earth, even when there was no immediate answer to his question.

DECISION OF GOD (Matt 27:51-28:20)

The burial of Jesus is preparation for his resurrection. Apocalyptic, revelatory events at the death of Jesus (Matt 27:45, 51-54) occur also at the resurrection (Matt 28:2-7) to confirm the reality of the risen body of Jesus. Fear is the normal reaction to extraordinary phenomena. The guards see and tremble in fear. The two women disciples receive an explanation of this event: the appearance and message of divine communication in the person of the angel is the very word and presence of the risen Jesus (Matt 28:5f, 9, 10). The prophetic message is fulfilled, once-for-all, and the prophetic word of Jesus is accomplished: "Do not be afraid . . . I go before you into Galilee, there you will see me" (Matt 28:7, 10).

DECISION OF THE SANHEDRIN

The chief priests and elders gather for one last time and take counsel. They decide to pay a sum of money to the guards, who then spread false testimony that the disciples stole the body. This paradoxically gives credence to the testimony that Jesus is risen from the dead. The presence of the guards and the message of the guards are reported until this day. The words of the Scriptures are fulfilled: the decision to accept or reject the message rests with us.

The revelatory events at the time of the death of Jesus are a radical reversal of all human decisions. God's decision conquers death. In the midst of darkness in the middle of day, the earth quakes and the dead rise. All these are biblical expressions of the action of God in the human condition—this world—and God's judgment for *life* over the people's judgment for death. The women who witness Jesus' death and burial testify for Jesus' resurrection (Matt 27:56, 61; 28:1). The presence of God in the risen Jesus comes in triumph and conquers the grave and the finitude of the human condition.

The women are commissioned to go to the disciples of Jesus and tell them that Jesus will go before them into Galilee. They are to return to the place from which they came, only to find a new beginning. The interpretation given by Jesus in the commission to the women offers a new relationship of Jesus to his followers. "Go! tell my BROTHERS . . ." (Matt 28:9-10).

Just as God is to be our Father as well as Jesus' Father (Matt 6:9), so Jesus is now our brother, which puts us into a new relationship with each other as well. The new relationship with all people and the new initiation into the community through baptism, the new teaching on morality and the new relationship to Jesus as Risen Lord, conclude the promise of God to Israel: "I am with you" (Matt 1:23) and "I will be with you all days, even until the end of the ages" (Matt 28:16-20). This is Israel's future, as Jew and Gentile peoples of God. All the blessings of the children of Abraham are fulfilled in Jesus.

Jesus *hands over* life in and through death. He *hands over* his own life so that others might have life. *Handing over* is the external act of the internal decision. Decision-making is contemporary language for a science that has been going on in the world since the beginning of time. It is formalized today in management and in business. It is a process that we all engage in as members of a community or of a society where individuals realize their interdependence. The life of a single individual is dependent upon and responsible to and for so many others. This is the contingency theory and the interdependence about which philosophers expound.

In Matthew's biblical terminology, *handing over* is deliverance. In the Passion narrative it is known as betrayal, denial, crucifixion. This is the dark side of life that ends in death as human beings perceive it. Paradoxically, the freedom to which all persons aspire derives from this process of *handing over*. In the ultimate turn of events, death really leads to a life eternal that God reveals to us in Jesus. It is the mystery or meaning of life and death; it is mystery because we still do not know WHY. Yet believing that life and death are both equally valid and important for the life that is eternal, we find meaning in the everyday events and the ordinary routine existence.

The light side of our decision-making process is exemplified in the Passion story as well. God raises Jesus to the life that is eternal. The Risen Jesus, as Lord, involves himself fully in ways we are unable to perceive when we *hand on* or *hand over* our life in faith to the other. *Handing over* is the dynamic act that identifies us with the same Spirit of life that Jesus bears and which was given to us at the beginning of all life in creation. *Handing on* the same Spirit of life in Jesus liberates us to see the earth break apart at the death and resurrection and release the bodies from the confines of the death that surrounds us. To *hand over* is a symbol of the earthliness that binds us, that refuses to liberate and free us, that limits our perceptions and hinders our movement through life. To *hand on* is the ability to release the earthliness that we see and the ability to decide for or against God. But the vision of the eye of faith moves beyond and through the human condition to the union of spirits and lives that are essentially one in the Spirit of God, the living God. Only Jesus could reveal this reality to us through death. To *hand over* is the way of life and death that we all journey. Decision-making prepares us "to see" with the inner eye of faith that our earthly life is only a different form of the Spirit of life that will never die. Life as spirit and truth is experienced in the moments of unity when we relate with others in daily encounters. It really does not matter if these moments are festive banquets where we enjoy the precious signs of adulation, praise and expensive perfumes and wines, or if we experience moments of libation with gall and vinegar by a life poured out in death.

The message of the gospel is the same. Our lives are all intertwined. Our decisions affect all other persons, places and things . . . for all time. Our actions flow from our choices and are a mere symbol of the mind's desire to unite with the other or separate ourselves from others as individuals or groups, society or community. We are left with the scene of death, the symbol of the cross where our union with God, our spirit and life with God, have been crossed over and intersected by our actions and our choices. To transgress is to trample on and usurp the rights and territory and space of the other human being. It may be in actual thievery or robbery, in communal life or personal life. The message of Matthew's Gospel goes beyond the individual to the communal understanding of the one life that permeates all of life. It is the one Spirit of God that has been *handed over* to us in Jesus, the one Spirit that will remain ever with the human spirit, without which we are dead. But the physical or earthly body is the external presence of "God-with-us." Even in death we now know that the person will never die. The person lives on, the Risen Jesus is with us "all days," even until the end of time.

This is only one aspect of the message of God's *handing over* life. Jesus is the witness of spirit and life *handed over* to the human condition. The way we are to continue this "good news" is by *handing over* the very same "life" to which Jesus testified. This is the prophetic message, and the authoritative and submissive obedience of Jesus' passion, death and resurrection life. The teaching is ours to *hand on* and literally *hand over*. The message is non-selective; it is all-inclusive. We are to teach ALL. One or other aspect of this total existence is not sufficient. Life is one long transforming process of *being handed over* or of *handing over*. The negative process is called "betrayal," the positive aspect "obedience." God has *handed over* to each one of us the same life principle or Spirit of life to be cherished and preserved in ways that make it possible for us to decide for or against "life." In this way we choose "life" or "death" (Deut 30:19). By witnessing to and participating in the same *handing over* of our very self to God and others, our decisions lead to life—even if they pass through situations that seem more like death.

The formulation of the teaching in the Passion narrative of Matthew's Gospel breaks down the barriers between individuals and communities. We are all in the position to betray or deny, even if we are intimate followers of Jesus. There is no one who is exempt from the possibility. We are also members of a community of believers in God who are dependent upon external forms of ritual beliefs. The community of believers is separated by the traditional observances that dictate what can or cannot be done by Law. The Law may be religious or civil. We aim at observing these laws so that we will not be incriminated on the "last day" in the END. But the laws can be observed and the decisions made according to the letter or legal observances only. We will not perform this service to the public today because it is a "religious feast" (Matt 26:5). It is a day of holy observance.But after the "passover" we will feel justified in condemning the JUST ONE. The ones who are perceptive to the internal voice (for example, Pilate's wife in her dream) are able to hear the word spoken in solitude, "Have nothing to do with this JUST MAN" (Matt 27:19). The decisions we make to put the innocent ones to death continue to plague us. We continue to act in a deceptive way. We still try often to cover up our actions that result from unjust decisions. We are continually *handing over* our personal decisions to the group to be executed. It is no longer a matter of judgment made on principles of what is just or unjust. It is the crowd or mob mentality that prevails. The crowds in frenzy ask for Barabbas, son of our earthly father and our brother in darkness, in place of Jesus, the Son of God, son of our heavenly Father, and our true Brother.

The decisions we make are very personal and have far-reaching results. The Jewish leaders *hand over* their decision to the legal courts. They in turn pass on the decision that is rightfully theirs to the world, the decision that should have been made in the light of the heavenly author of life. The decisions that are made with "God-with-us" are decisions that require a simple YES or NO! The truth needs no further explanation. Oaths are not needed (Matt 5:33-37). We need not swear before God or call upon God "out there" to justify what we say because it already flows from the internal voice of faith that indeed "God is with us"—to decide and to do that which we are committed to do by our faith-stance. We are believers in the PRESENCE: we are believers in the life that has been given to us to hold in highest regard and to cherish as the one means to the end. The END is to show forth and witness that "God-with-us" as the risen Jesus, is the Spirit of life that will continue to spur our confidence, our believing, hoping and loving of all others as God has loved us.

God does not condemn. The judgment we make on others is the same judgment we mete out to ourselves (Matt 7:1-5). The questions we ask in probing our mind, the questions we voice in our interactions with others, require answers. But the answer we give is the decision we have made in the process of *handing over* our answer to light or to darkness: to the Spirit of God or to the spirit of the world. The one who speaks with the spirit of the world will find accusation, will find judgment and reasons for condemnation. The one who speaks with the Spirit of God will live this message, knowing that Jesus is always with us.

"This man says: he will destroy this temple and rebuild it in three days" (Matt 26:61). The reasons may be personal: "This man says he is Son of God" (Matt 27:43). Judgment is our own perception of ourselves. We never ask: what do you mean when you say you are son of God? Is your perception the same as mine? What do you mean by saying you will destroy this temple? There are always several ways of interpreting these statements, depending upon the persons who make the judgment. In the course of the Passion narrative, Jesus does not make judgments. Jesus interprets for his own disciples. Jesus gives reasons for his action. Jesus is free to see the behavior of his friends from the perspective of God, the perspective of the END and the goal of the action. Judgment is something which belongs in the *hands of God*. It is for us to believe that a person is doing this action out of love, like the woman who anointed the head of Jesus, from the perspective of the END—the goal of the action: "she has anointed me for my burial" (Matt 26:12). The end is to be with God here and hereafter, the goal of our human existence. Neither is the person judged by Jesus. The reasons for one's actions reside in the mind of the person, and the answers to questions are one's very own: "You have said it!" responds Jesus (Matt 26:64).

Jesus deals with his most intimate followers and with the legal authorities in the same way! What is your decision? This is your answer; and you are to live with your decision and your own judgment. The person of Jesus does not judge. All judgment is left to the end of time (Matt 25).

The worth and the value of actions are set down before others. God does not punish in this world; the tragedies we witness in life are not God's condemnation. They are not a sign of God's disfavor nor of God's judgment upon the whole human race. The earth does not open and quake to swallow up and consume the soldiers and the crowds of people who condemned Jesus. The earth quakes and releases from the confines of the earth the bodies of those who have died (Matt 27:51-53).

God's deliverance allows us to make our decisions in freedom. Yet we live or die in the process. Judas was able to decide and act; he was also able to repent and confess his sin. But he was not able to forgive himself. His own despair took his life. By contrast, Peter was able to forgive himself, and thus he could accept Jesus' forgiveness. If God is God, we are not asking God to make us and determine us: we have been made and created free to decide for or against God, self, others. Peter knew that the Lord knew his heart. He knew the Lord expected the rejection; he had already predicted that it would be so. Yet Jesus neither alienated nor condemned Peter. Perhaps an interior dialogue with the Lord in all our actions frees us to perform all of them in the light of the living, loving Lord. The mistakes that we make, the good that we do, the sin that separates us from ourselves and others will never separate us from God who silently stands in readiness to accept our return. We *hand over*, once again, the person of self to God; we do not *hand over* the sin! In this way we boldly proclaim our sorrow.

Epilogue

The Christian community has the same needs and the same desires or questions today, that people had two thousand years ago. The search for unity, peace and happiness in the homes, hearts and lives of each one of us is the same. This quest may be called the desire for salvation, but there is little that changes from age to age in the innate desires of persons to be whole, to be one with God, oneself and others. Because this quest continues in the world, we conclude that the kingdom of heaven has arrived in Jesus, but it is not yet fully realized. The tension that is experienced is often spoken of as END-TIME tension. It prompts one to look ahead to the end, the goals that have been set for our lives. We have peace and happiness and the realization of God's presence with us, but not at all times. And so we struggle to effect that change in our world which will do away with the situations of conflict that are death-dealing rather than life-producing.

To strive to bring about this new situation by systemic changes alone results in failure because we have not realized that at the root of all action and being is the heart. Our hearts are continually making choices for our lives but the presence of Jesus in our world has not been sufficiently realized, nor has the presence of his word in our minds and hearts been sufficiently heard to recognize that Christians are called to live by faith and not by sight. The Christian is called to believe that God's kingdom is realized in Jesus. His throne name, Emmanuel "God-with-us," has taken flesh in a community of believers who live in hope and expectation of his coming. The form that this God-presence has taken is radically different from the type of kingdom and savior that Israel expected. When the promise was not fulfilled according to these expectations, Israel could not "see," could not "believe" and could not accept the way God chose to live out the word or promise—to be with us. Jesus, the form of God's presence, needs to be reimaged, reinformed and given a meaning that satisfies the hopes and realizations of a lifetime.

Each one of us bears a very small portion of that time which is called life-time. Time with God is life eternal and never ceases. We are given the opportunity to choose to see Jesus present with us again in this short span of time so that we can live out our lives in relationship with him, here and now, in and through others—if we so desire and choose.

When, as children of the kingdom, we leave the rule, the power and the decisions for our world to the infinite power and determining will of God, the command to teach becomes a lesson in forgiveness. Jesus has shown us the desire of God to be with us; the possibility of repentance reveals that God is not alienated nor separated from us. Are we able to choose life in all its circumstances of change and painful transition in order to manifest the kingdom of heaven here on earth because we believe that God is with us?

Since the Second Vatican Council there has been tension in the Church between those who wish to retain the old traditions in fidelity to Jesus and those who believe they are being called to renew and rededicate the Church in light of the revelation of

Jesus as experienced in the interpretation of Scripture for our day. Some of the problems facing the Church have to do with the old traditional ways and the new thinking: the transition from the hierarchical Church to one of greater participation of the laity; the move from a male-dominated Church to one of greater involvement of women; a change from the old concept of an unchanging morality to one of greater understanding of the problems of our day, i.e., homosexuality, married clergy, the need to change religion from an institution to a 'way of life.' There is need today for the Christian community to participate more fully in the world community or society. In order to resolve these tensions we try to listen to what Jesus is telling us in the Scriptures and try to follow his instruction, knowing that discipleship is costly. But we also have hope founded on the message that Matthew tried to instill in the early Church: Jesus is the fulfillment of the promise—the fulfillment of all our expectations. This is the gift of our faith.

The tensions experienced in Matthew's Jewish Christian community are not peculiar to the early stages of Christianity. They have been with the Church, the people of God, throughout all of its history. At times they are more deeply experienced and more wrenching than at others. Today is such a time! Once again we are given the challenge and the opportunity to be the gift of God's presence, the revelation of his Word and Deed in our world. This is Matthew's message to us and it is our response to Jesus, Israel's promise and expectation. It is the greatest mission for all time: the responsibility to allow the kingdom presence, "God-with-us," to be known and loved. This is God's forgiveness and our peace. To live in a like manner is the spirituality of WISDOM.

Suggested Readings

W.D. Davies, *The Sermon on the Mount.* Cambridge: Cambridge University Press, 1966.

D.J. Harrington. *Gospel According to Matthew.* Collegeville: The Liturgical Press, 1983.

J.P. Meier. *Matthew.* New Testament Message 3. Delaware: Michael Glazier, Inc., 1980.

_____ *The Vision of Matthew: Christ, Church and Morality in the First Gospel.* New York: Paulist Press, 1979.

D.Senior. *Invitation to Matthew.* Image Books. Garden City: Doubleday, 1977.

_____ *The Passion of Jesus in the Gospel of Matthew.* Delaware: Michael Glazier, 1985.

_____ *What Are They Saying About Matthew?* New York: Paulist, 1983.

BIBLICAL INDEX

OLD TESTAMENT

NEW TESTAMENT

188   *Index*